MY
LITTLE
GARDEN
IN
EDEN

MY LITTLE GARDEN IN EDEN

Reconciled and Living in the Will of God

DR. MIKE DUFFY

ISBN - 979-8-9894314-8-9 (paperback)
ISBN - 979-8-9894314-9-6 (ebook)

Unless otherwise stated, all Scripture quotations come from the King James Version. Public Domain.

Editing by Gretchen Doolittle
Cover design and typesetting by Jenneth Leed

TABLE OF CONTENTS

INTRODUCTION

ℐ remember when I first started reading the Bible how overwhelming it was to me. I did not understand it. It seemed so disconnected and foreign to what I knew about life. Some of the words were strange and unfamiliar to me. I can only imagine that many others felt the same way.

Now, decades later, through study and spiritual growth, my understanding is far more mature, and the wisdom God has given me to apply his Word to my life context is much greater. I have a greater understanding of how it is all connected, although I am the first to admit there is much more for me to learn. The complexity of learning and doing the will of God has come into a much simpler focus for me. While profound enough in its academic width and depth to challenge the mind of the most ardent, scholarly theologian, the Bible's simplicity is available for all common folks like me. And that is what I hope to convey to all who read this book.

I also hope to make clear that a person's faith, or religion, is not to be confined to a building and an hour or two on a Saturday, Sunday, or some other designated day of the week. True biblical faith is about a relationship, not a religious behavior.

The Bible is so practical and thorough. God's Word reveals the Creator's intent to the created (that's you and me) and provides the power for each of us creatures to fulfill the Creator's intent. It also reveals the power and pathway of God's process of reconciliation and transformation of a "lost soul" who is spiritually dead in trespasses and sins to a "saved sinner" who is spiritually alive in Christ. This book is about my understanding of God's will for mankind and God's will for you and me! I have grown to think of God's will for me as "My Little Garden in Eden." This will make more sense to you as this story unfolds. You may see your little garden in Eden too!

GOD KNOWS YOU AND LOVES YOU. HE HAS A LOVING DESIRE FOR YOUR FUTURE.

For I know the thoughts that I think toward you, saith the Lord, thoughts of peace, and not of evil, to give you an expected end. Then shall ye call upon me, and ye shall go and pray unto me, and I will hearken unto you. And ye shall seek me, and find me, when ye shall search for me with all your heart. — Jeremiah 29:11-13

CHAPTER 1

CREATED IN THE IMAGE OF GOD

One of the first things we learn in the Bible is that man is created in the image of God. This is such an important place to begin. To help develop our understanding, consider this text from the first chapter of the Bible:

> And God said, Let us make man in our image, after our likeness: and let them have dominion over the fish of the sea, and over the fowl of the air, and over the cattle, and over all the earth, and over every creeping thing that creepeth upon the earth. So God created man in his own image, in the image of God created he him; male and female created he them. And God blessed them, and God said unto them, Be fruitful, and multiply, and replenish the earth, and subdue it: and have dominion over the fish of the sea, and over

the fowl of the air, and over every living thing that moveth upon the earth. Genesis 1:26–28

What does it mean to be created in "the image of God"? Good question! Being created in the image of God means that man—in construct, image, and likeness—is in some way like God the Creator. That concept is difficult to wrap one's mind around. I am not sure any of us will fully comprehend the importance of all this until we get to heaven. But this is what the Bible is telling us. Suffice it to say, God made mankind unique above all other life that he created. No other creation was created in God's image, but mankind was. So let's consider the following thoughts and strengthen our own understanding.

Man has a moral component. The first man was created righteous and innocent in a dispensation before sin existed in the world. The first two chapters of Genesis tell us about God's creation. Because there is no negative influence in these chapters, we begin to understand God's original intent, or we might say "his perfect will." Sin does not show up until Genesis 3.

During this age of innocence, the first man knew what was right, and he did what was right. He exercised his free will in a way that pleased God—every time! Therefore, he was innocent. Not a trace of guilt because of sin. With a clear conscience, man could stand in the presence of the Holy God and communicate with him. Simply put, the "created one" could fellowship with the "Creator"! This helps us understand a little bit of God's original plan for mankind. By the way, that plan is still God's plan today. He wants you and me to be in fellowship with him—participating in an active, vibrant relationship.

Being created in the image of God, man has a **material element**, the **body**, which might be considered man's temporal housing. His body was "formed from dust of the ground" (Genesis 2:7) and will return to dust after physical death (Genesis 3:19). For now, however, the body is the earthly clay vessel that serves as home to man's soul and spirit, the other two key elements of man.

Man has an **immaterial element** called his **soul** (Genesis 2:7). God made man to be a living being or person. This reality is evident when we can make a statement like **"I am a person; I have a body."** The body is the outer man, and the soul is the inner man. The Bible says that God breathed life into us, and we became a living soul. The soul is everlasting, but the body is temporary.

There is an interesting passage of Scripture that teaches us how the body and soul separate at the time of physical death: Genesis 35:16–20. In this passage, Rachel is giving birth to her son Benjamin. In the birthing process, she dies. Verse 18 points out that her soul departed her body, and then her husband buried her body in a grave and marked it with a stone. Her soul continued to live somewhere. This pattern is still common practice nowadays even though the event described there happened thousands of years ago. Man dies and is buried, and a memorial stone is placed on the grave that serves as the final resting place of his body.

Man's soul is made up primarily of his intellect, emotions, and will and is often referred to as "the inner man." Mentally, he is rational and volitional, meaning he can reason and make decisions. Emotionally, he has feelings and thus forms opinions. His intellect and emotions inform his free will as he faces the issues of life; then, with his will, he makes determinations and decisions.

The soul is often referred to in Scripture as the "**heart of the man**." King Solomon taught his son this wonderful truth about the relationship between the heart and the will: "Keep thy heart with all diligence; for out of it are the issues of life" (Proverbs 4:23). This "keeping of our heart" is one of the most critical issues of the Christian life. Solomon was saying to his son to be diligent about "guarding" or protecting his heart (intellect and emotions) from wrong influences because when an issue of life came along, the condition of his heart would impact his choices. If his heart was "godly" when facing an issue, he would make a godly response or choice. However, if his heart was "carnal" or ungodly, his choices would also be carnal or ungodly.

By being in the image of God, man has **a spirit** so he **can relate to** and **fellowship with God, who is spirit** (John 4:24). This is man's most important relationship. Knowing God in this personal way is the essence of eternal life (see John 17:3 for Jesus' definition of eternal life). Man was created a "social being," and so, he was capable of having fellowship and participating in a relationship with the Creator. God found pleasure in man's fellowship, and loving God is the greatest commandment for man. Relationship is at the heart of God's original intent.

Man was created. He did not evolve from some lower form of life. The history of mankind from generation to generation is recorded in the Bible. Your ancestors are people, not monkeys, tadpoles, or some abstract residue from an explosion. You are designed by the Creator for a purpose he has determined. The first two chapters of Genesis provide a vast knowledge of God's creation. The understanding of these two chapters provides a solid

YOU ARE DESIGNED BY THE CREATOR FOR A PURPOSE HE HAS DETERMINED.

foundation upon which any person can build a fruitful and fulfilling life. These opening chapters of the Bible are worthy of man's deepest dive in pursuit of truth. They are rich in knowledge about who we are, where we came from, and the world around us in which we live today.

"**Male and female created he them**" (Genesis 1:27). God determined each person's gender to fulfill his purpose in their life, in their marriage, in their family, and in the communities in which they would participate. In a marriage, the man is the husband (a male person[1]), the woman is the wife (a female person[2]). The eternal Word of God is settled on this issue! Unfortunately, and to their own detriment, many in the world around us are not settled on this issue. They choose to believe someone or something else. Unfortunately for them, what someone believes does not change the truth. God's Word is forever settled in heaven (Psalm 119:89)!

A special note of caution here, popular culture has greatly attacked this truth about gender in recent years. Be careful not to believe the lies that false teachers and false prophets have propagated, even though false teachers may claim to be who the majority of the people believe. Since the beginning of mankind, the enemies of God have been undermining and attacking truth. The destruction of the family is a primary goal of the enemies of God, and this destruction is the source of much of the confusion in the culture today. Recognizing the cultural battle today and connecting it to God's original intent in Genesis will help us understand the spiritual warfare that has raged for most of the history of mankind. The battlefield is truth!

GOD DETERMINED EACH PERSON'S GENDER TO FULFILL HIS PURPOSE IN THEIR LIFE.

I have always been amazed at the immense scope of God's creative genius and his wonderful imagination in that no two people are alike. Each of us is unique in body, soul, and spirit. King David expressed this same amazement: "I will praise thee; for I am fearfully and wonderfully made: marvellous are thy works; and

EACH OF US IS UNIQUE IN BODY, SOUL, AND SPIRIT.

that my soul knoweth right well" (Psalm 139:14). David acknowledged God's creative work and that he was part of it.

Just consider for a moment your own family, your circle of friends, and the community in which you live, and you will see what I am talking about. There is only one of me and only one of you! And it is so by God's choice!

CHAPTER 2

GOD'S INTENT FOR MANKIND

God created an ideal environment in which mankind would dwell. The Bible teaches us that it was God who planted a garden on the eastside of Eden and he placed the first man there. Look closely at some key words in the following two verses, from which we can learn some very important things that influence our spiritual life:

> And the Lord God **planted** a **garden** eastward in **Eden**; and there **he put the man** whom he had formed. And out of the ground made the Lord God to grow every tree that is pleasant to the sight, and good for food; the tree of life also in the midst of the garden, and the tree of the knowledge of good and evil. Genesis 2:8–9

Planted—God, with obvious intention, "planted" or

"established" a place for man to live. He willed it and created it! Planting the garden was intentional.

Garden—God made an "enclosure, a garden."[3] I like to think of this as the "context" God intended for me to occupy. God designed the context in which the man would live.

Eden—The garden was located on the eastern side of Eden. The name *Eden* means "pleasure."[4] So considering this enclosure, or garden, which was God's delight, we can certainly say, "This is God's will. It is what he desires and where he finds delight."

He Put the Man—This became the first habitat for man after the creation. The specific site is unknown to man today; however, many generally consider it to be somewhere in or near what we call the Fertile Crescent today. We'll discuss the "where" a little deeper in the book.

In verse 8, we learn that mankind is created for **God's purpose** and **pleasure**, not man's own purpose and pleasure (see also Revelation 4:11). This is so vitally important to understand! If we do not begin with this truth as our foundation, by misunderstanding God's intent, mankind quickly goes his own way and, in so doing, goes astray. We need to understand and embrace the truth that God has a "will" for every man, including a will for your life and a will for mine. That should be encouraging to all of us because it also means we are part of his big plan! That is exciting to me! It also says a lot about how God values each of us. We are so privileged to live in a day when we can see much of God's plan by reading the Bible. We see his original intent.

We see the birth and history of Israel, God's chosen people. We learn of fulfilled prophecy that has been documented in the history books of mankind. What God said came to pass! We can see how God worked in the lives of people thousands of years ago and learn how God is working in our lives today. God has a huge master plan for mankind, and we are part of it!

If you spend time pursuing God's will, you will not have to imagine or create a will or plan of your own. You will discover it in God's Word. Consider the following:

> And the Lord God took the man, and put him into the garden of Eden to dress it and to keep it. And the Lord God commanded the man, saying, Of every tree of the garden thou mayest freely eat: But of the tree of the knowledge of good and evil, thou shalt not eat of it: for in the day that thou eatest thereof thou shalt surely die. Genesis 2:15–17

As we saw in chapter 1, God's stated purpose for mankind in creation was to be fruitful and multiply, to replenish the earth, to have dominion over the animal kingdom, and to subdue the earth—bringing it into subjection. This purpose placed man in a position of responsibility and authority as a steward of some of the possessions of God. He was to manage and lead as God directed him. We see clearly in this passage that God "placed" and "commanded" the man.

Adam's first responsibilities included dressing and

keeping the garden of Eden. For Adam, working would be an avenue for both fulfillment and provision as he obeyed God. He would fulfill his purpose of pleasing God. He was to be a protector, like a watchman of sorts. So we could say that the man was both the gardener and the guard as a steward of God's stuff.

God also established some boundaries in the garden. One tree was "off limits" to Adam—the tree of the knowledge of good and evil. Violating the boundaries would be a transgression against God's purpose for mankind and the command of God and, as such, bring sorrow to Adam. Let me encourage you at this point to stop and meditate on this truth for a moment. God did not have a long list of rules, or as some say, "the dos and don'ts." There was a single prohibition not to eat from the tree of the knowledge of good and evil. God did not intend on making Adam's life miserable! Rather, God wanted Adam to enjoy his life in the garden and their relationship.

By man choosing to fulfill his responsibility in obedience to God, he would glorify God with his life, fulfilling God's purpose for himself. Sounds easy enough, right?

I think we could accurately say that God set man up to successfully fulfill his will. This was the perfect opportunity for mankind. In the translation of God's Word into Latin, the Vulgate translated the word *garden* as *paradiso* to describe it. The garden of Eden certainly would be a paradise before the fall of man! The word *paradise* is used three times in the New Testament. Think about the place, *paradise*, that these three verses reference.

This first instance is Jesus responding to the request of one of the thieves who was crucified with Jesus. After this convicted criminal turned to Jesus in repentance and confessed his saving faith in Jesus as the Savior, Jesus responded this way: "Verily I say unto thee, Today shalt thou be with me in **paradise**" (Luke 23:43, emphasis mine). Instead of spending an eternity separated from Christ after enduring a long, agonizing death on the cross, the repentant thief would be in *Paradise* with Jesus that very day! What hope! What relief!

In the second passage where the word is found, the Apostle Paul is describing the experience of a man, likely himself: "How that he was caught up into **paradise**, and heard unspeakable words, which it is not lawful for a man to utter" (2 Corinthians 12:4). He was speaking of a heavenly place he had been privileged to see. What he saw was so overwhelming that he could not put it into words what it looked like! He had never seen anything on earth like it! It was a paradise that left him speechless!

Finally, the Apostle John speaks of the eternal dwelling place of God, a place where all who are saved will live forever. "He that hath an ear, let him hear what the Spirit saith unto the churches; To him that overcometh will I give to eat of the tree of life, which is in the midst of the **paradise** of God" (Revelation 2:7).

Think about it. The place of God's pleasure and delight is where God wants us to be for all of eternity! The paradise of God. It will be the same paradise that Adam lost because of his disobedience. Sin separated Adam from the paradise God desired and designed for him. And now, he wants us to experience his pleasure and delight as we journey down life's pathways with the pearly gates in view.

CHAPTER 3

MY LIFE IS MY LITTLE GARDEN IN EDEN

I think you will agree, we live in a big world and a vast universe. It would certainly be easy to get lost in this bigness! What most people are concerned with, however, is their own life, their own little context in this vastness. One might ask, **"What is my purpose, and what am I to be doing?"** Or, they may wonder, **"Where am I supposed to be?"** These are some of the questions I deal with regularly while helping young believers grow in the grace and knowledge of the Lord Jesus Christ.

My life and my life's context are unique to me, and yours is unique to you. My life and context make up the unique place that God made for me and is where God wants me to be. That is the place where I fellowship with him and fulfill his pleasure. This is **my little garden in Eden**. My fellowshipping with God is part of what God created to bring pleasure to himself.

As I occupy my little garden in Eden, I can communicate regularly with God, further discovering his will for me. When I walk in faith and obedience there, I am living out my life in the "**will of God**." This is the reality of Philippians 2:13: "For it is God which worketh in you both to will and to do of his good pleasure." (God's will, his choice, delight, and intent.[5]) This is also where I experience the joy and fulfillment God intends for me!

Well, where is that garden? It is not just a fixed geographical location on planet earth. God can move me to whatever place on the planet he wants me to occupy. My garden is the place where I am, wherever that is. This is where God is engaging with me and where my personal walk with God happens! It is my spiritual life, the part of me that connects with God in relationship. Wherever I am, I am to do what I know God wants me to do—whatever that is and however it may turn out, I just do it! I trust God and obey him.

I have a body, and I have a soul, and I am a spiritual being, created in the image of God! I can talk to him, and he talks to me. This communication takes place on a spiritual level and is often manifest in my physical life as I trust and obey his Word and the leadership of his Holy Spirit. I will talk more about this in the coming chapters, but it needs to be said that the Holy Spirit of God, who lives in me as a born-again child of God, teaches me God's Word, and

I am able to comprehend it because, as the Bible says, it is "spiritually discerned" (1 Corinthians 2:14). I am now spiritually alive and able to understand it. The Holy Spirit is teaching my spirit the mind and heart of God. Those who are still spiritually dead in their trespasses and sin do not understand because they have no spiritual discernment. This condition, however, can be fixed by the grace of God! We will talk more about that, too, in the chapters to come.

Now being alive in Christ, I can talk to God. He wants to hear from me. He wants to see that I sincerely "believe that he is, and that he is a rewarder of them that diligently seek him" (Hebrews 11:6). He wants me to acknowledge my dependence on him and express my needs and desires to him just as any child should want to do with their father. They do so with an innate understanding that he is their provider and protector. A father finds delight in his child's dependence! This is what praying is about, communing with God in the relationship he reestablished when he saved us from our sin and gave us eternal life.

He also wants me to express gratitude for the mercy and grace he provides daily. My praise of him glorifies and pleases him. As others hear or see me do this, it magnifies the Lord! Through all of this, God is fulfilling his purpose in me.

CHAPTER 4

THE WILL OF GOD FOR MY LIFE

$\mathcal{W}$hat does fulfilling God's will for my life look like? I remember hearing this statement many years ago: **"God's will: nothing more, nothing less, and nothing else."** This is certainly a noble goal—truly finding God's purpose for one's life and then fulfilling it without being distracted or led away by the enticements of the world or the attractions to self-serving personalities. Jesus, himself, is the perfect example for us in that he came to do the will of the Father (see Luke 22:42), and then as he neared the end of his earthly life, he could say, "I have glorified thee on the earth: I have finished the work which thou gavest me to do" (John 17:4). Staying focused on our purpose is what God desires of us too.

Also, our life is unique and designed for discovering and fulfilling the will of God. Like Adam's role in the age of innocence was to "dress and keep" the garden, my role is to do the same in **my little garden in Eden** today. I am a steward of the gift of life and the relationship God has given me with him. I must make it the priority of my life to care for it. After all, the garden belongs to God. He planted it and placed me here. This means I must understand what God's will is and then execute it as a steward of God in a manner that would be pleasing to him, and in so doing, I will accurately project a right opinion of who God is to those watching my life.

One could say of the garden God has for me that it is to be my life's environment and experience. I was created for it. God was intentional. Like Adam, I, too, went astray and was lost in sin, but I have now been reconciled to God and brought back to **my little garden in Eden** and am ready to do the will of God. I have been born again into the family of God! My life has gone from once being spiritually dead in trespasses and sin to now being alive in Christ. I have another opportunity to fulfill God's will in my life. This is why I exist! It is my purpose! It must be my life's pursuit! The following is how others have said virtually the same thing.

THE WHOLE DUTY OF MAN

In any context, the purpose of a summary statement is to help one recognize and focus on the important point that is being made. The following statements were made by men who had been placed in very significant roles of leadership by God. The statements were made to the nations they were leading. Consider, for a moment, their exhortations.

In his final opportunity to address the nation of people he had led for more than forty years out of Egypt and through the wilderness, Moses summed up the prospect for God's blessing. He didn't rehearse all that he had accomplished in his time leading them. He focused on what they would need to do going forward as they entered the promised land. He said:

See, I have set before thee this day life and good, and death and evil; In that I command thee this day **to love the Lord thy God, to walk in his ways, and to keep his commandments and his statutes and his judgments,** that thou mayest live and multiply: and the Lord thy God shall bless thee in the land whither thou goest to possess it. But if thine heart turn away, so that thou wilt not hear, but shalt be drawn away, and worship other gods, and serve them; I denounce unto you this day, that ye shall surely perish, and that ye shall not prolong your days upon the land, whither thou passest over Jordan to go to possess it. I call heaven and earth to record this against you, that I have set before you life and death, blessing and cursing: therefore choose life, that both thou and thy seed may live: **That thou mayest love the Lord thy God, and that thou mayest obey his voice, and that thou mayest cleave unto him: for he is thy life, and the length of thy days:** that thou mayest dwell in the land which the Lord sware unto thy fathers, to Abraham, to Isaac, and to Jacob, to give them. Deuteronomy 30:15–20

The message was easy to understand and simple enough for the people to embrace. God's people were to live life God's way and, in doing so, would secure his blessing. For ease of remembrance, we might say it like this: The people were to **love, trust, and obey!**

Next, consider Joshua, God's chosen leader to succeed Moses. In his conquest of Canaan, Joshua implored the people to serve God as he shared his understanding of man's personal responsibility in this statement:

> But take diligent heed to do the commandment and the law, which Moses the servant of the Lord charged you, **to love the Lord your God, and to walk in all his ways, and to keep his commandments, and to cleave unto him, and to serve him with all your heart and with all your soul.** Joshua 22:5

Joshua's message certainly was not complex or too difficult for the average man on the street to comprehend. Joshua made it clear that it was man's responsibility to make a personal choice. He would have to trust God and obey.

 **LOVE - TRUST - OBEY!**

Then, King Solomon summed up the whole of man's life when he made this statement:

> Let us hear the conclusion of the whole matter: **Fear God, and keep his commandments: for this is the whole duty of man**. For God shall bring every work into judgment, with every secret thing, whether it be good, or whether it be evil. Ecclesiastes 12:13–14

Once again, not a difficult truth to understand and embrace. Performing the will of God without the help of God (God's grace) would prove to be quite difficult. Trying to navigate life without God would be foolish and fatal.

I LIKE TO THINK OF GOD'S WILL THIS WAY: LEARN IT, LOVE IT, AND LIVE IT!

Micah the prophet of God said to the rebellious nation of Israel:

> He hath shewed thee, O man, what is good; and what doth the Lord require of thee, but to **do justly, and to love mercy, and to walk humbly with thy God**? Micah 6:8

Once again, a simple message with an exhortation to exercise one's will. We can see a common thread in these passages—trust and obey! I like to think of man's pursuit of God's will this way: We are to **learn it, love it, and live it**!

For us believers in the church age, Jesus summed up our responsibility with two commandments.

> But when the Pharisees had heard that he had put the Sadducees to silence, they were gathered together. Then one of them, which was a lawyer, asked him a question, tempting him, and saying, Master, which is the great commandment in the law?
> Jesus said unto him, **Thou shalt love the Lord thy God with all thy heart, and with all thy soul, and with all thy mind**. This is **the first and great commandment**. And the **second** is like unto it, **Thou shalt love thy neighbour as thyself**. On these **two commandments** hang all the law and the prophets. Matthew 22:34–40

Do these exhortations not help us to see what God's priority for mankind is? Certainly they do! He wants us in a proper relationship with him and fulfilling our God-given purpose, as he has determined it.

Even as I read these again, I am struck with the realization that each verse is very personal because everyone would have to exercise their own will to embrace the exhortations. Their personal future would be influenced by the choices they made. Just like how our relationship to God is today—it is very personal.

The simplicity in these passages creates an incredible burden of personal responsibility. It is not unusual for man to deflect from this responsibility and accountability by shifting the focus to what others should be doing. Consider the following classic passage in John 21:20–23 and you'll see an example. After enjoying a lunch on shore after some of the disciples endured a long overnight fishing trip, Jesus began to speak to Peter by asking some probing and challenging questions. Three times Jesus asked, "Peter, do you love me?" Peter answered the best he could and finally understood what Jesus was saying to him. He got the message! Then this:

> Then Peter, turning about, seeth the disciple whom Jesus loved following; which also leaned on his breast at supper, and said, Lord, which is he that betrayeth thee? Peter seeing him saith to Jesus, **Lord, and what shall this man do?**
>
> Jesus saith unto him, **If I will that he tarry till I come, what is that to thee? follow thou me.** Then went this saying abroad among the brethren, that that disciple should not die: yet Jesus said not unto him, He shall not die; but, **If I will that he tarry till I come, what is that to thee?**

Peter was given explicit instruction by Jesus what he was to do and was even told how he would die. That, in itself, is quite incredible to me! Upon hearing this, Peter looked about and then asked Jesus what John was supposed to do. Jesus made it clear that what God had for John was none of Peter's business. Peter was to follow the will of God for Peter, not John.

This certainly illustrates for us the personal nature of our relationship and the unique task God has for us in his will. It also reveals how foolish we are today when we deflect from obedience by using excuses like Peter did. We should pursue an understanding of God's will, then do it! When we trust and obey, we are empowered by the grace of God!

What is it that makes it so difficult to embrace and execute the will of God in our lives? Perhaps a regular time of meditation about our own responsibility and opportunity with God would help us identify and remove the trash or noise that so easily distracts us! Some might call it a time of personal devotion. It would help us clean up our own "environment." You know, dress and keep it!

CHAPTER 5

HOW THE FALL OF MAN IMPACTS MY LIFE

fter all the good news we read in Genesis 1 and 2, we get some bad news in chapter 3. At this point, I encourage you to read Genesis 3 in its entirety. This chapter tells us the circumstances surrounding the disobedience of Adam and Eve, God's response to it, and how Adam's disobedience plunged the human race into sin and, with it, much sorrow. Having a basic understanding of what transpires there will provide you with many of the answers to questions you have about your own life. In a sense, this is where life begins AGAIN! This time, however, man no longer has the bliss of innocence, but now, he is saddled with a sinful nature and a keen conscience that recognizes it.

WHAT IS SIN?

Our soul feels a sense of guilt when we sin against God. In the New Testament, we find the word *sin* is the original

Greek word *hamartia*.[6] This word means, "A particular evil deed, or to wander from or violate God's law." In the Old Testament, the Hebrew word means "to go wrong" or "to miss the mark."

While there are many things we believe or think to be sin, these following Bible verses clearly state things that God says "**are sin**":

- An high look, and a proud heart, and the plowing of the wicked, **is sin**. Proverbs 21:4

- The thought of foolishness **is sin**: and the scorner is an abomination to men. Proverbs 24:9

- And he that doubteth is damned if he eat, because he eateth not of faith: for whatsoever is not of faith **is sin**. Romans 14:23

- Therefore to him that knoweth to do good, and doeth it not, to him it **is sin**. James 4:17

- All unrighteousness **is sin**: and there is a sin not unto death. 1 John 5:17

What becomes clear in the Bible is that any behavior against the will of God **is sin**. God has an intent and an expectation for mankind. That is clearly illustrated in the garden of Eden when God created and placed man there. It was Adam's disobedience to God's command that was sinful. In Adam's soul, he exercised his will against the ways

IF MAN'S TRUTH IS COUNTER TO GOD'S TRUTH, IT IS A LIE, AND IT IS SIN.

of God. His exercise of will against God was sin, and because of Adam's sin, there was a catastrophic consequence.

It is vital that we understand that **mankind does not establish the moral code**! God has already established it. He determined what was right, or righteous. Man must choose whether or not to embrace and follow God's determination. I have heard many defend their errant ways by saying something like, "Well, that's my truth!" or "I just don't see it that way!" If man's truth is counter to God's truth, it is a lie, and it is sin. It is true that man is free to live the way he chooses to, but this choice does not mean he establishes the rules or sets the moral code. He either chooses God's way or his own way. What man chooses to do is always on display for God and will be judged by God. God's judgment is driven by his code of righteousness. Living our life is the real contest of "truth or consequences." Do it God's way or pay the penalty!

THE WAGES OF SIN

God established a penalty for sin. Think about that for a moment. God established the rules and then articulated the consequences for those who break the rules. He respected the ability to "choose" that God had given man when he created him. By the way, this is a good lesson for anyone in leadership, particularly with a responsibility like parenting children. When God established this sin penalty, he also established consequence. That consequence was not simply a punishment for bad behavior, it was intended to be an incentive for good behavior.

The Apostle Paul helps us understand the penalty when he writes to the believers in Rome.

> For when ye were the servants of sin, ye were free from righteousness. What fruit had ye then in those things whereof ye are now ashamed? for the end of those things is death. But now being made free from sin, and become servants to God, ye have your fruit unto holiness, and the end everlasting life. **For the wages of sin is death**; but the gift of God is eternal life through Jesus Christ our Lord. Romans 6:20–23

The wages one receives, earns, or deserves for being a sinner and sinning is death. Consider the definition of the word *death* in the Bible, provided by Blue Letter Bible: "Properly, an adjective used as a noun death (literally or figuratively):—X deadly, (be…) death. . . . In the widest sense, **death comprising all the miseries arising from sin, as well physical death as the loss of a life consecrated to God and blessed in him on earth, to be followed by wretchedness in hell.**"[7]

The penalty that God established affects the sinner personally. God had his prophet Ezekiel clearly state:

> **The soul that sinneth, it shall die.** The son shall not bear the iniquity of the father, neither shall the

father bear the iniquity of the son: the righteousness
of the righteous shall be upon him, and the wickedness
of the wicked shall be upon him. Ezekiel 18:20

From this passage, we can learn our personal
responsibility comes with a personal accountability
to God. If I sin, I pay the
price! This is the ultimate **WITH PERSONAL**
expression of the "sowing and **RESPONSIBILITY**
reaping" principle. **COMES PERSONAL**
ACCOUNTABILITY!
Do you remember God's
instruction in the garden of Eden to Adam while he was in
a state of innocence? Don't eat of the fruit of the tree of
the knowledge of good and evil. If you do, you will surely
die. The decree of God set a boundary for mankind. If in
exercising his God-given privilege of choice man violated
the boundary, he would suffer the consequence.

And the Lord God commanded the man, saying, Of
every tree of the garden thou mayest freely eat: But
of the tree of the knowledge of good and evil, thou
shalt not eat of it: **for in the day that thou eatest
thereof thou shalt surely die**. Genesis 2:16–17

God determined Adam's penalty for disobedience would
be death.[8] This was to be both a spiritual death and physical
death. Adam's fellowship with God was broken, and he
began to die physically.

Spiritual death is separation from God. Adam would be exiled from the garden of Eden and would be living outside God's original intent and will for Adam. As a result, Adam would not be living in "paradise." He would be away from fellowship with God. He would know both good and evil. He would suffer consequences that would make his life miserable and difficult. The Bible speaks of this curse in Genesis 3.

From the day Adam's exile began, he would learn that the enemies of God are always on the offense. They did not want Adam to provide the pleasure to God that God had intended. These enemies would be manifest throughout the Scriptures as Satan, also known as the serpent and the devil; the cursed world and its anti-God practices and philosophies; and the flesh of the man that would pervert the appetites God had created in him.

THE SIN NATURE

As much as we may not like to admit it, we need to understand and embrace the truth that we are born with a sinful nature—a bent or tendency toward sin. Sin comes naturally to us. Sin is often appealing, and sadly, we are desirous of engaging in it. In order to avoid sinning, we need to be intentional, choosing what is good and right while rejecting what is evil and wrong. We must exercise our will toward righteousness, which is God's original intent for us.

The rubber meets the road when we understand the foundational appetites God has given us, and we learn how to manage those appetites. Let me give you a couple examples to consider:

Power, having dominion, or rule (re: Genesis 1:26): We have been given the power of dominion—the ability to rule or subjugate the animal kingdom, including the fish, the fowl, and every creeping thing on the earth. We can exercise this authority and power responsibly, or we can abuse it.

This certainly can be abused if we don't keep that appetite in check. We are to exercise this power for righteousness' sake. We must not abuse the power at the expense of the animal kingdom. King Solomon gave this example to his son: "The slothful man roasteth not that which he took in hunting: but the substance of a diligent man is precious" (Proverbs 12:27).

The pursuit of power, like the pursuit of riches, can certainly contribute to the perversion of God's intent for man.

The sexual appetite (re: Genesis 1:28, 2:18): While often we think of this only in the context of procreation, or having kids, it seems the primary purpose is for developing the intimate relationship between a husband and wife in marriage. This creates a close, knowledgeable relationship unrivaled anywhere, except in our relationship with our Creator.

The coming together of husband and wife may, but not always, result in a child. Consider the psalmist's acknowledgement: "Lo, children are an heritage of the Lord: and the fruit of the womb is his reward" (Psalm 127:3). Children are "assigned by" or given to us by God. They are a reward given by him.[9] And let's not avoid the obvious, fulfilling this appetite is the way God has chosen for man to procreate. However, while physical intimacy between a husband and wife is wonderful, outside those boundaries, it is an abuse of the appetite.

Accomplishment or achievement (re: Genesis 1:28): In the first chapter of the Bible, God told man to "be fruitful and multiply." Being successful would become a driving force for mankind. It is a wonderful thing to observe and recognize the power of God working in us and through us to accomplish something. Just think about working at something you love or enjoy, then seeing the fruit of that effort. We often call that fulfillment.

We get in trouble when we start seeking "personal fulfillment" or "I did that!" Self-gratification seeks its own reward and not the reward of God. Cain and Abel's sacrifices illustrated that self-gratification has been a problem for a long time. Abel offered to God in the way that God had instructed. Cain chose to do his own thing. He offered what he produced as a means of trying to impress God. That was wrong.

The hunger appetite for food and water (re: Genesis 1:29, 2:16): These are life-sustaining appetites. They feed and fuel the intricate systems God created in the human body. Each of these appetites must be controlled within the will of God, such as eating a balanced diet, striving to move our body each day, and controlling our appetite by indulging in treats in moderation (1 Corinthians 6:12). Having a sin nature, however, causes us to lean away from God's will, so we pervert these appetites toward pleasing our own selfish desires instead of pleasing God.

These are just a few examples of the "nature" of sin and its influence on man. Some have identified a list they call the "Seven Deadly Sins": pride, greed, lust, envy, gluttony, wrath, and sloth. A couple of thoughts here. First, this is not an exhaustive list! They seem to be foundational categories that lead to a host of sinful behaviors. Any behavior contrary to God's will is sinful.

Second, these "deadly" sins are not the only deadly sins! The penalty for all sin is death. In our excuse-making response to our guilt of sinning, we often try to diminish the severity of one sin over another. You know, the little white lie isn't as bad as the big lie! In God's economy, a lie is a lie, and it is sin.

We must battle the effects of the fall of man every day. It is as though we live in a sea of sinful corruption, and our presence is adding to it. Isaiah the prophet of God wrote these difficult words as part of his prayer for God's people:

But we are all as an unclean thing, and all our righteousnesses are as filthy rags; and we all do fade as a leaf; and our iniquities, like the wind, have taken us away. And there is none that calleth upon thy name, that stirreth up himself to take hold of thee: for thou hast hid thy face from us, and hast consumed us, because of our iniquities. Isaiah 64:6–7

Notice that Isaiah uses first person pronouns and, by doing so, considers himself part of the group he was addressing. We are all sinners! God's Word says it, and that settles it.

In a practical sense, this is why seeking to have "high self-esteem" is such a problem for man. People doing an honest evaluation of their own life will ONLY conclude that all have sinned and fallen short of the glory of God. We are all sinners! And we are all in need of a Savior who will pay the death penalty on our behalf to be reconciled to God.

What man needs to seek is an accurate estimation of self. That is possible to find. But high self-esteem is nothing more than a mirage. One never realizes it. It is a vain pursuit.

TEMPTATION

In our understanding of our sin nature, we must also realize the draw of temptation. Mankind faces a constant battle with the temptation to resist or rebel against God. In the book of James, we see a significant passage about temptation and its effect on mankind:

Blessed is the man that endureth temptation: for when he is tried, he shall receive the crown of life, which the Lord hath promised to them that love him. Let no man say when he is tempted, I am tempted of God: for God cannot be tempted with evil, neither tempteth he any man: But every man is tempted, when he is drawn away of his own lust, and enticed.

Then when lust hath conceived, it bringeth forth
sin: and sin, when it is finished, bringeth forth death.
James 1:12–15

Overcoming temptation brings blessing or happiness. It
does so because we understand we have pleased God. Notice
that temptation does not come from God, and we will all
face some temptation in life. This temptation comes from
our own desires. As sinners by nature, we have a natural
inclination to desire sinfulness. That is sad but true! We need
to understand that truth and embrace it, or we will never
get victory over temptation.

When we entertain the temptation, that is we do not
resist and reject it, sin finds a beginning point in our heart.
It is then manifested through our sinful behavior. That
separates us from God. The point is, we should address sin
at the temptation stage, immediately. As soon as we recognize
the temptation, we should reject it. This is why we need to
have "standards" in our lives. I will say more on this later.

The Apostle Paul offers us additional instruction
as he encourages the believers in the church at Corinth
of their ability to overcome the temptations of life that
they would face:

Wherefore let him that thinketh he standeth take heed
lest he fall. There hath no temptation taken you but
such as is common to man: but God is faithful, who
will not suffer you to be tempted above that ye are able;

but will with the temptation also make a way to escape, that ye may be able to bear it. 1 Corinthians 10:12–13

We should never develop the mindset that we are spiritually invincible or that we are no longer susceptible to temptation or able to fall into sin. There is a common quotation used by many Bible teachers that says, **"The best of men, are men at best!"** (The true authorship of that quotation is unknown.) However, how true that is!

When it comes to temptation, we are best served by humility. We recognize that we are saved but truly only saved sinners. Our pride will make us more vulnerable to yielding to the temptations we face. We must fear sin and flee temptation!

The good news is that whenever we face temptation, God provides the way to escape it. Often that way is the

WE MUST FEAR SIN AND FLEE TEMPTATION!

Holy Spirit reminding us of truth that already is in our hearts. The psalmist wrote, "Thy word have I hid in mine heart, that I might not sin against thee" (Psalm 119:11). It is so important to memorize God's Word and meditate on it. It is like resupplying our defense arsenal so the Holy Spirit has the ammunition needed to combat the next battles we face. When well supplied, we can bear the temptation and come away with victory.

THE DEVIL AND HIS DEVICES

The devil is clever and active. We must always be on guard for his presence and devious plots. In Paul's second letter to the Corinthian church, he writes:

> To whom ye forgive any thing, I forgive also: for if I forgave any thing, to whom I forgave it, for your sakes forgave I it in the person of Christ; **Lest Satan should get an advantage of us: for we are not ignorant of his devices.** 2 Corinthians 2:10–11

Paul understood how the enemy worked. The devices Paul speaks of are Satan's sinister thoughts and plans. In the context, Paul knew that the devil would try to trap someone by having them hold on to vengeance or bitterness instead of graciously granting or getting forgiveness.

In his pastoral epistle to Timothy, Paul exhorted Timothy to teach in such a way that his listeners might "come to their senses and escape the snare of the devil" (2 Timothy 2:26 NKJV). The Bible will teach us how Satan works to wound or destroy our lives.

In Ephesians 6:11, Paul tells us that we are to put on the whole armor of God that we might be able "to stand against the wiles of the devil." The word *wiles* means "tricks." The devil uses tricky "tactics" or "schemes" or "strategies." These are carefully arranged plans to deceive and outwit others. The devil's primary work includes deception, disappointment, discouragement, doubt, and division. You can see this throughout Scripture. The scriptural admonition to us as we maintain our gardens in Eden is simple:

> Submit yourselves therefore to God. **Resist the devil, and he will flee from you.** Draw nigh to God, and he will draw nigh to you. Cleanse your hands, ye sinners; and purify your hearts, ye double minded. James 4:7–8

I have to remind myself regularly that I am living in the devil's domain. It is as though we are playing an away game. This world is not our home. The devil has all his resources available to make life difficult for God's people. We are not to engage him, rather we are to resist him with God's truth. He hates that, but eventually, he flees. You can see how Jesus overcame the temptations of the devil in Matthew 4:

> Then was Jesus led up of the Spirit into the wilderness to be **tempted of the devil**. And when he had fasted forty days and forty nights, he was afterward an hungred. **And when the tempter came to him**, he said, If thou be the Son of God, command that these stones be made bread.
>
> But he answered and said, **It is written**, Man shall not live by bread alone, but by every word that proceedeth out of the mouth of God.
>
> Then the devil taketh him up into the holy city, and setteth him on a pinnacle of the temple, And saith unto

him, If thou be the Son of God, cast thyself down: for it is written, He shall give his angels charge concerning thee: and in their hands they shall bear thee up, lest at any time thou dash thy foot against a stone.

Jesus said to him, **It is written again**, Thou shalt not tempt the Lord thy God.

Again, the devil taketh him up into an exceeding high mountain, and sheweth him all the kingdoms of the world, and the glory of them; And saith unto him, All these things will I give thee, if thou wilt fall down and worship me.

Then saith Jesus unto him, **Get thee hence, Satan: for it is written**, Thou shalt worship the Lord thy God, and him only shalt thou serve.

Then the devil leaveth him, and, behold, angels came and ministered unto him.

Each time the devil tempted Jesus, Jesus said, "It is written." He was quoting Bible truth as his defense mechanism. After three unsuccessful attempts, the devil fled.

We need to use this same strategy. We don't resist the devil in our power, we use the power of God to chase him away.

CHAPTER 6

RECONCILING TO GOD & RESTORING MY RELATIONSHIP

$\mathfrak{I}$ cannot even begin to imagine the heartbreak and heartache God experienced when he exiled Adam and Eve from the garden he had prepared for them. That thought stirs my conscience regularly about my own life and behavior. It makes me wonder what hurt I may cause God to experience.

Before sending Adam away, God showed him that there would be a way for reconciliation and redemption, giving Adam hope. God provided a blood sacrifice in the garden as a covering for Adam and Eve and their nakedness: "Unto Adam also and to his wife did the Lord God make coats of skins, and clothed them" (Genesis 3:21). What a merciful act!

This act foreshadowed the work of the coming Redeemer, the Messiah, the Lord Jesus Christ. (See Hebrews 9:16–22.) He, too, would shed his blood and die to provide a covering for our sin and a pathway back into a relationship with God.

In God's provision for Adam and Eve, there was HOPE for us too! Hope of reconciliation is the primary message we can learn throughout the rest of the Bible. The primary message of the Bible is the story of God redeeming mankind and bringing him back into fellowship, we could say back to "God's Eden," his place of perfect delight and pleasure, and man's occupation of his own place within the will of God, his own little garden in Eden.

I sometimes wonder if Adam, as he was walking away from the garden, didn't say to himself, "**I wish I hadn't done that**." Undoubtedly, he had some regret and was certainly ashamed. It makes me understand that in Adam's soul there was a conflict between what he knew was right and the temptation to exercise his own will in a way that would please himself instead of God. This seems to be the battle all mankind experiences many times a day and for their entire lifetime. Adam probably thought, "**If I could just do this over I would do it a different way!**"

I love how the Apostle Paul explained reconciliation as he wrote these words to a repentant church at Corinth.

Therefore if any man be in Christ, he is a new creature: old things are passed away; behold, all things are become new. And all things are of God, who hath reconciled us to himself by Jesus Christ, and hath given to us the ministry of reconciliation; To wit, that God was in Christ, reconciling the world unto himself, not imputing their trespasses unto them; and hath committed unto us the word of reconciliation.

Now then we are ambassadors for Christ, as though God did beseech you by us: we pray you in Christ's stead, be ye reconciled to God. **For he hath made him to be sin for us, who knew no sin; that we might be made the righteousness of God in him.** 2 Corinthians 5:17–21

Through repentance and faith in the finished work of Jesus Christ, a person is reconciled to God. In God's economy, that person is covered with the righteousness of Christ! God no longer sees their disqualifying sin. Their sins are blotted out! They are under the blood! He only sees the imputed righteousness of Christ, metaphorically, wearing robes of righteousness that are white and clean. God orchestrated the process and series of events to bring us back into relationship with him. Oh, how he loves you and me!

REPENT AND BELIEVE

The pathway to reconciliation begins with these two words: *repent* and *believe*! People often think these two words are inseparable, or they are simply parts of one simple act called *faith*. While closely linked in Scripture, I see them as two definable acts of a person's will: repenting (having a change of mind) and then believing (trusting). I find some clarity on this issue by considering a passage in the book of Acts describing the Apostle Paul's ministry in Ephesus. There had been a confrontation by Paul about sinful behavior and the need of the people for a Savior. Confrontation is necessary, but it is not easy. Notice the separate acts of repentance and believing by faith in this text and then consider the object of those acts:

> From Miletus he [Paul] sent to Ephesus, and called the elders of the church. And when they were come to him, he said unto them, Ye know, from the first day that I came into Asia, after what manner I have been with you at all seasons, Serving the Lord with all humility of mind, and with many tears, and temptations, which befell me by the lying in wait of the Jews: And how I kept back nothing that was profitable unto you, but have shewed you, and have taught you publicly, and from house to house, Testifying both to the Jews, and also to the Greeks, **repentance toward God**, and **faith toward our Lord Jesus Christ**. Acts 20:17–21

First, their repentance was "toward God." Sorrow for their violation of God's law was expressed to, or toward, God. After all, it was God who man sinned against. This repentance was a recognition of their wrong behavior, and then they took responsibility for committing the sins, denoting a change of mind. It is akin to finally admitting personal responsibility by stating, "**I know it was wrong and I wish I had not done it, but I did! I do not want to**

repeat this error." This must be a sincere desire in the heart of the sinner. Their repentance was toward God the Father. They were turning from their selfish sinfulness and turning to God, whom they had sinned against, desiring reconciliation.

Then, believing the remedy God had provided, they received God's gift of salvation through the Lord Jesus Christ. "Faith toward" our Lord Jesus Christ is when people embrace the truth that the life, death, and resurrection of Jesus Christ paid the penalty of sin they owed, a penalty they were unable to pay themselves, and that this sacrifice by Christ was satisfying the justice of God. They were now sincerely trusting that this finished work of Jesus was sufficient to satisfy God's righteous demands and, in doing so, would bring them back into fellowship with him. They believed the payment Jesus made was for them, and they embraced that truth, receiving Christ as their own Savior.

What leads a man to repentance is an awareness or understanding that he has sinned against God, and he is now truly sorry for it. He is sorry to the degree that he wants to make his error right and is willing to turn from his wrong behavior toward godliness or right behavior. In this process, the sinner often experiences grief, or a heaviness in his heart, that he has behaved in a way that displeases God. He is guilty and knows it. His awareness usually comes from being confronted with the truth of God's Word. This often happens during the presentation of the gospel message or an exhortation from a caring Christian. This is considered "godly sorrow." He is not only sorry that he got caught in his sin but also that his sin offended God, and he is ashamed that it did offend God. This kind of sorrow and shame comes from the heart of man in sincerity, and the Bible tells us it is what "leads" him to repentance.

It is possible to have a different kind of sorrow. One is sorry they were caught in their sin, but they are not grieved about its impact on God or their relationship with God. The Bible identifies this as a "worldly sorrow."

Consider the following passage that addresses the issue of repentance and distinguishes the two kinds of sorrow.

> For though I made you sorry with a letter, I do not repent, though I did repent: [They were confronted with truth.] for I perceive that the same epistle hath made you sorry, though it were but for a season. **Now I rejoice, not that ye were made sorry, but that ye sorrowed to repentance**: for ye were made sorry after a godly manner, that ye might receive damage by us in nothing. **For godly sorrow worketh repentance to salvation** not to be repented of: but **the sorrow of the world worketh death**. For behold this selfsame thing, that ye sorrowed after a godly sort, what carefulness it wrought in you, yea, what clearing of yourselves, yea, what indignation, yea, what fear, yea, what vehement desire, yea, what zeal, yea, what revenge! In all things ye have approved yourselves to be clear in this matter. Wherefore, though

I wrote unto you, I did it not for his cause that had done the wrong, nor for his cause that suffered wrong, but that our care for you in the sight of God might appear unto you. 2 Corinthians 7:8–12

Consider the outcomes of this godly sorrow as articulated in the previous passage. Paul could determine their sincerity by these responses:

- **Created Diligence**: The Corinthians had an attitude change about sin, and the Apostle Paul describes it as, "What carefulness it wrought in you." This means to have an eager and earnest interest in what is going on in your life and around you and to take a serious approach to life and your relationship with God. While being aware of the possibility of a recurrence of sinful behavior, they took steps to avoid offending God again.

- **Caused a Clearing of the Conscience**: The apology to God clears one's conscience—"What clearing of yourselves." His new plea is like saying, "I don't want to sin, and I am not going back to that sinful life!" One takes responsibility for his actions, acknowledges he was wrong, and now seeks God's forgiveness. He doesn't try to continually justify his wrong behavior. He accepts, by faith, the forgiveness God is

AS RECONCILED BELIEVERS, WE CAN LIVE OUR LIVES WITH A CLEAR CONSCIENCE!

granting as he confesses his sin to God. This is clearly stated in 1 John 1:9, "If we confess our sins, he is faithful and just to forgive us our sins, and to cleanse us from all unrighteousness."

Think of the opportunity here! As reconciled believers, we can live our lives with a clear conscience! That should motivate any true Christian.

- **Developed a Righteous Hatred of Sin**: Godly repentance creates a passionate anger toward sinful behavior—"What indignation." This seems to become a natural reaction when one truly repents. A person sees how ugly sin is and how awfully it has affected his relationship with the Lord. He will now speak out against it. He will not entertain it. He no longer has a neutrality or tolerance for sin in his own life.

- **Produced a "Fear Phobia"**: Having a reverential fear of God, believers are alarmed or frightened that they may continue a sinful behavior, which is appalling to them—"What fear." This mentality is a healthy respect for the power of sin and the weakness of our own will. This is a positive fear in that this fear causes us to develop standards of behavior that support our efforts to stay right with God. We put boundaries on ourselves to protect us and to prevent harmful things from invading our human experience.

- **Generated a Spiritual Hunger and Drive**: The people had a new longing for right behavior in their own life and in the lives of others—"What vehement desire." Character counted! It now mattered! This kind of desire drives one to study God's Word with a new attitude. Believers want to learn what behavior needs to go and what new behavior needs to replace it. They "put off the old man" and "put on the new man" (Ephesians 4).

- **Shaped a Passionate Zeal for God**: The true repentant person wants to know God better and adore him more—"What zeal." Believers want to honor and please him. They want others to know him too. Some would say the person was "on fire for God"! That would certainly be a description of this level of zeal.

  This issue reminds me of my time as the director of a Bible camp. Teenagers would come to a week of summer camp apathetic to the things of God or even lost in their sin. After receiving a heavy concentration of Bible teaching and preaching and seeing peers who loved God and were serving him, many turned to God from their sinful ways and put their faith in Christ. Others would restore their strained relationship with God. Upon returning home, one would often hear, "They are on fire for God." There was this renewed zeal!

- **Fashioned a Spirit of Restitution**: Desiring to see justice, believers should attempt to make restitution to those they had harmed—"What revenge!" Other versions will use the word *vindication*. These believers were willing to accept their punishment without making an argument or excuse and then make restitution wherever and whenever possible. Instead of saying, "I am sorry. I didn't mean to do that," they say, "I am sorry. I will not do that again." There is ownership and commitment, not excuses, after acknowledgment. That demonstrates a different spirit.

The apostle would tell the Corinthian believers of the fruit of their repentance: "In all things ye have approved yourselves to be clear in this matter." The slate was clean, the forgiveness was granted, and they could now move forward in their relationship with the Lord.

A man by the name of Robert Smith said, "True repentance has a double aspect. It looks upon things past with a weeping eye, and upon the future with a watchful eye."[10] This is a great characterization of the repentant heart. Godly sorrow leads to repentance, not something to be repented of! This kind of sorrow is fruitful and beneficial to the repenting sinner, and it is pleasing and acceptable to God.

On the other hand, the Apostle Paul gives warning about an insincere act of repentance. He says it begins with a "worldly sorrow." It seems as though this kind of sorrow is really dealing with the exposure of one's sin issue to influence man for their own benefit or advantage, rather than seeking forgiveness and reconciliation with God.

This worldly sorrow says, "I am not sorry that I have broken God's heart, I am sorry that I got caught, and I will now have to pay some consequences." It is selfish and self-centered! And worse than that, this kind of sorrow works death.

MY LITTLE GARDEN IN EDEN

In contrast to godly sorrow, the fruit of this kind of sorrow is quite different. One's attitude toward sin remains unchanged. They have no fear of sin. Their attitude toward righteousness remains unchanged. It isn't important to them. They are ashamed to acknowledge Christ because they still have a guilty conscience. The life change is only one of outward conformity and usually short-lived. The reformation is temporary and incomplete because it is done in one's own strength, or perhaps better said, their weakness. Worldly sorrow does not satisfy the righteous demands of a holy God.

Isaiah the prophet of God was preaching to a wicked and rebellious people calling them to repentance. His message certainly reveals to us the true spirit of genuine repentance:

> Seek ye the Lord while he may be found, call ye upon him while he is near: **Let the wicked forsake his way**, **and the unrighteous man his thoughts**: and **let him return unto the Lord**, and he will have mercy upon him; and to our God, for he will abundantly pardon. For my thoughts are not your thoughts, neither are your ways my ways, saith the Lord. Isaiah 55:6–8

Repent and believe was the message of Jesus. As Jesus began his earthly ministry, his first message was "**repent: for the kingdom of heaven is at hand**" (Matthew 4:17). Repentance was the first response Jesus expected from the people to whom he was preaching. If they were to be reconciled to the Father, they would have to have a change of mind and a trusting faith.

The Apostle Paul, preaching on Mars' hill in Athens to a group of cultural leaders, declares God's expectation for man after they heard the truth:

> And the times of this ignorance God winked at; **but now** [now that they had been confronted with truth] **commandeth all men every where to repent**: Because he hath appointed a day, in the which he will judge the world in righteousness by that man whom he hath ordained; whereof he hath given assurance unto all men, in that he hath raised him from the dead. Acts 17:30–31

And don't miss this truth in the passage: The resurrection is "proof" that there is an appointment and that Jesus will be the judge of all of mankind! This act of sharing truth is an act of God's mercy, driven by God's love for us. Man must respond to it in repentance for deliverance, and if not, in his rebellion, he will face judgment. There will be no neutral position once confrontation has taken place.

Before we leave this section, I thought it would be helpful to understand a little more about man's conscience. In situations we have just considered, the conscience acts like a data processor.

WHERE DOES OUR CONSCIENCE RESIDE?

How does our consciousness impact our daily relationship? To begin to answer these questions, let's start by getting the definition of the word *conscience*.

Conscience—co-perception, i.e., moral consciousness. "The soul as distinguishing between what is morally good and bad, prompting to do the former and shun the latter, commending one, condemning the other."[11]

Some synonyms of *conscience* are *perception*, *mindfulness*, or *awareness*. Conscience is our inner voice, perhaps that which stays in communication with the Holy Spirit, which would mean it is part of our "spirit." We were created body, soul, and spirit. We might look at our conscience as our data processor, using data from our intellect and emotions to help us exercise our will in making choices. This is consistent with 1 Corinthians 2:9–14 which teaches us how God's Word is spiritually discerned.

Consider the Apostle Paul's letter to Pastor Timothy describing those who lose their discernment where he uses the term *conscience*. He's describing those who ultimately depart from what they once believed and embrace that which is the opposite. Their data processor is malfunctioning because it is seared—cauterized, resulting in crusting and loss of function.

Now the Spirit speaketh expressly, that in the latter times **some shall depart from the faith, giving**

heed to seducing spirits, and doctrines of devils;
Speaking lies in hypocrisy; **having their conscience
seared with a hot iron**; Forbidding to marry, and
commanding to abstain from meats, which God hath
created to be received with thanksgiving of them
which believe and know the truth. 1 Timothy 4:1–3

So what can we learn from this?

When we begin to doubt God's Word or refuse to believe
God, our conscience is affected, and this mental attitude
eventually manifests itself in our behavior, leading to a strain
in our daily relational walk with Christ. It's not that we just
stop believing, but we also start believing the wrong thing.
The theological term we often apply to this shift is *apostacy*.
When one apostatizes, his whole worldview changes from
God-centered and eternal to man-centered and temporary.
So consider this: If you turn away from God, don't expect
the result in your life to be godliness. It will be just the
opposite—godlessness.

History is replete with examples of apostacy. The pull
of sin and the power of the adversaries are always at work
trying to interrupt man's relationship with God. Think
about it. Israel transitioned from a relationship with God
and following him to a religion that crucified the Savior. In
America, the Ivy League universities that we established to
train young men for the ministry of God's Word (over 52
percent of Harvard grads in the first 100 years of its history
went into pastoral ministry[12]) transitioned to bastions of
liberalism, rejecting God and his Word.

The following is an excerpt from my book *The Tragedies and Triumphs in an Alcoholic's Family*:

History records for us the natural occurrence of apostasy in institutions and organizations. Consider the Ivy League Universities. Most, if not all, started for the purpose of training people to minister the Gospel of Jesus Christ. Harvard was started in 1638, just 18 years after the Pilgrim's landed at Plymouth Rock. In Harvard's Rules and Precepts adopted in 1646 these essentials were articulated:

"Everyone shall consider the main end of his life and studies to know God and Jesus Christ which is eternal life. Seeing the Lord giveth wisdom, everyone shall seriously by prayer in secret seek wisdom of Him. Everyone shall so exercise himself in reading the Scriptures twice a day that they be ready to give an account of their proficiency therein, both in theoretical observations of languages and logic, and in practical and spiritual truths..."

Today, each of these schools has apostatized into godless institutions of liberal thought.

Organizations like the Boy Scouts of America, Girl Scouts, 4-H, and many churches are only a shell of what they once were as they have left their Godly foundations. Apostasy has robbed them of their original purpose and impact."

I was a both a cub scout and a boy scout when I was growing up. I still remember the Boy Scout Oath that we recited at the beginning of each meeting. It went like this: *"On my honor I will do my best to do my duty to God and my country and to obey the Scout Law; to help other people at all times; to keep myself physically strong, mentally awake, and morally straight."*

By the way, in case you don't remember that morality, that is, what is right and what is wrong, was established by God! It is set forth in His Word, the Bible. He is the moral authority! He is the one who sets the moral compass!

My point here is to remind us that maintaining a relationship with God as our first priority will always be challenged. We must discipline ourselves to make him our priority. Even the strongest Christian among us is prone to fail in this area. Why? Because we are weak in our own strength!

This makes me think of the prophetic passage in Revelation 2. Here is a church that seemed to be doing all the church things right. But then! Jesus chastised them for "leaving their first love." My pastor recently described this phrase, saying, "The people were in love with the love of God, but they had left their love for God." I understood this to mean they had abandoned the loving of the person of God while continuing to embrace the concept of God's love. Relationship had become religion! Such a subtle transition.

If we are honest about this, just look at a typical congregation today. You may find a bunch of churchgoers who are busy about the work of the church but have no time for a relationship with God. It seems like there are many Marthas and not so many Marys. (See Luke 10). My experience tells me that underlying all this, there is a guilty conscience and an unfulfilled life. If you find this to be the case, you likely have some reconciling work to do with God.

FAITH

What is faith? Whenever I hear that question, my mind goes back to a story I heard early in my Christian life. It goes like this:

A man was once asked, "What do you believe?" He responded by saying, "Well, I believe the same thing the pastor believes."

Dissatisfied with the response, the questioner asked, "Well, what does the pastor believe?" And the man said, "The pastor believes the same thing I believe."

And then, in frustration, the questioner asked again, "Well, what do you and the pastor believe?" And the man responded, "Well, we both believe the same thing!"

The conversation ended there! The questioner never found out what the man truly believed.

What do you believe? Or should we say, who do you believe?

When we speak of believing by faith, what do we mean? I like to define saving faith like this: **Faith is taking God at his Word and acting accordingly.** Someone once said, "Faith is not an emotion, it is a decision to stand on God's Word." How true that statement is! The Apostle Paul, writing to the believers in Rome said as much, "So then faith cometh by hearing, and hearing by the word of God" (Romans 10:17). Saving faith is not only what you believe but who you believe. Paul was stating that people developed faith by hearing what God said and then embracing it. There are sincere people all over the world who believe in someone or something other than Almighty God and his Word.

Let's continue this thought and incorporate repentance into the conversation, because it is repentance that begins our relationship. The act of repentance denotes a change of mind and direction. Consider this verse, "There is a way which seemeth right unto a man, but the end thereof are the ways of death" (Proverbs 14:12). Amazingly, it is repeated almost verbatim two chapters later: "There is a way that seemeth right unto a man, but the end thereof are the ways of death" (Proverbs 16:25). These verses describe much of mankind today. People who are just going about life, unaware and not caring about what lies at the end of life's journey. They are just doing their own thing.

Try to visualize the thought in these verses of a man walking down life's pathway, believing with all his heart that he is doing right and that he is heading in the right direction. What he doesn't know as he journeys on is that at the end of this pathway is death and destruction. His sinful life is headed for catastrophic ending in an eternal hell, even though he is sincere in his belief about his journey.

Why would he continue this journey? Who and what is he believing? Ask yourself, "What does this person need?" What he needs is for someone to step into his path, interrupt his journey, and warn him about his direction and the danger that lies at the end of the trail. That person challenges him to stop and turn to a different way. If he does make a change, his arrival at the end of his journey will be paradise. In other words, he can now change his mind about his direction in life, choose a better option, and decide to turn to that different pathway. If he were to take the person's word and make the change, that would be a picture of faith and repentance.

We, too, were once headed for destruction, not even recognizing the danger until someone stepped into our path and presented us with the warning—the knowledge of sin and its penalty—and then told us of the opportunity we would have through the gospel of Jesus Christ to reconcile to God. Upon hearing and heeding the warning, we made an intentional choice to change direction and put our trust in the finished work of the Lord Jesus Christ for salvation. Now what lay at the end of our life's pathway is not death and destruction, it is eternal bliss in our relationship with Almighty God in the eternal city, heaven. True repentance will result in observable change by the repentant and creates a different, much better outcome!

So at this point in our reading, let's consider some foundational truths that tie some of these thoughts together.

First, what you believe doesn't change the truth! Man can

choose what and whom to believe, but that does not change what is the real truth. He or she will ultimately hang their hat on a nail of belief and then live with it, experiencing either the blessings or curses of that choice. The universal questions on the mind of men are **where did I come from, why am I here, and where am I going?** The answer will be found in the truth. Does the body of truth that you have placed your faith in answer any or all these questions?

How would you answer the following question? **What is your source of truth?** There are many answer options to this question. Some trust what they have been taught—education; others trust what they have observed—experience; some follow men—mankind; others follow movements—groups of thinking.

One of the most significant issues regarding any source of truth is authority. For example, the Christian Bible believer's authority is in "**Thus saith the Lord God.**" So before you put your faith in someone or something, you might want to ask some questions. "Where does their authority come from?" You might follow up with this question, "Who gave the person or writing the authority?" or "In what way or to what degree, am I accountable to that authority?" and "Do I believe there will there be a day of reckoning?" These are questions for which you need definitive answers because God has already determined when judgment day will be and who the Judge will be. Taking God at his Word by faith is how one reconciles with God and begins or restarts his personal relationship with God.

WHY YOU SHOULD BELIEVE THE BIBLE

In her poetic masterpiece, "How Do I Love Thee? (Sonnet 43)," nineteenth-century author Elizabeth Barrett Browning answers that question with, "**Let me count the ways.**"

Why should you believe the Bible? Well, let us count the ways! There are many reasons I believe the Bible, and you may want to consider each of them from your own perspective. Here are some:

The Bible is self-authenticating. "So then faith cometh by hearing, and hearing by the word of God" (Romans 10:17). When we realize that a belief we hold has already been validated in the Bible, it builds our faith. Early in my Christian experience, I thought I needed to prove to others that the Bible was true and right. It did not take long for me to realize that the Bible defends itself. It stands as truth and is willing to be challenged. It always wins the challenge!

The Bible states that it is God's Word. "Sanctify them through thy truth: thy word is truth" (John 17:17). Jesus Christ in his high priestly prayer to the heavenly Father made this request. How much more clearly could it be said? The Bible is God's message to mankind!

The Bible is inspired by God. (It is God-breathed.) "All scripture is given by inspiration of God, and is profitable for doctrine, for reproof, for correction, for instruction in righteousness" (2 Timothy 3:16). The Apostle Paul writing to Pastor Timothy made this statement. God gave us Scripture so we could know him, how he works, and what his will for us is—for our benefit.

Whenever I think about the inspiration of God's Word, I imagine him standing nearby and speaking these words to me. He is breathing them out. I hear the words and feel his breath.

The Bible is authored by the Holy Spirit of God and was penned by holy men of God. "We have also a more sure word of prophecy; whereunto ye do well that ye take heed, as unto a light that shineth in a dark place, until the day dawn, and the day star arise in your hearts: Knowing this first, that no prophecy of the scripture is of any private interpretation. For the prophecy came not in old time by the will of man: but holy men of God spake as they were moved by the Holy Ghost" (2 Peter 1:19–21). The Apostle Peter wrote this to believers. We might look at this as God being the author and dictating to his secretary or a stenographer. It was God's message, penned by his secretary, and delivered to us.

The Bible is a collection of writings, sixty-six different books, written over a period of 1,600 years, by more than forty authors, on three continents, and using three different languages.

Although these writings were done independently of each other, there is an amazing continuity, and these books are in complete harmony! That would be considered one of the most amazing coincidences in the history of mankind if it were not from God! I consider it one of God's miraculous works. Many have tried to prove the Bible to be wrong or to contain contradictions only to find they were the ones who were wrong.

Gilbert West was included in Samuel Johnson's *Lives of the Most Eminent English Poets*. As a student at Oxford, West set out to debunk the Bible's account of Christ's resurrection. Instead, having proved to himself that Christ did rise from the dead, he was converted. West published his conclusions in the book *Observations on the History and Evidences of the Resurrection of Jesus Christ* (1747). On the fly-leaf he had the following printed: "Blame not before thou hast examined the truth."[13]

Every prophecy of Scripture has come true or is positioned to come to pass. One of the most recent would be the reforming of Israel as a nation in 1948. Consider this passage:

And in that day there shall be a root of Jesse, which shall stand for an ensign of the people; to it shall the Gentiles seek: and his rest shall be glorious. And it shall come to pass in that day, that the Lord shall set his hand again the second time to recover the remnant of his people, which shall be left, from Assyria, and from Egypt, and from Pathros, and from Cush, and from Elam, and from Shinar, and from Hamath, and from the islands of the sea. And he shall set up an ensign

for the nations, **and shall assemble the outcasts
of Israel, and gather together the dispersed
of Judah from the four corners of the earth**.
Isaiah 11:10–12

God never fails, and all of his prophetic Word will
be fulfilled. Sometimes it is difficult for people to accept
prophecy. I get that. They have not seen it, so they won't
believe it—yet! They might even be labeled a "doubting
Thomas." Well, everything else in the Bible has been true,
why would prophecy be the exception? Just as certain as there
is a sun, moon, and stars and as certain as the first coming
of Jesus happened like all the prophecies said it would, so
too, will the second coming of Jesus Christ happen!

In Jeremiah 16:15, God promises that the Israelites
will dwell in "their land that I gave unto their fathers," and
Ezekiel 36 describes the incredible transformation of the
land itself into a major agricultural center. It has become
one of the breadbaskets of Europe. Israel is among the larger
producers of fruits in the world!

**The principles established by God are observable
today.** For example, "What goes around, comes around!"
While not stated in the Bible in that precise way, the principle
is observable in life. What the Bible does teach is, "Be not
deceived; God is not mocked: **for whatsoever a man
soweth, that shall he also reap**" (Galatians 6:7). This
is the principle of "sowing and reaping." You plant a seed

of corn, and it grows corn! Plant some lettuce seeds, and you get lettuce. If you sow a bad spirit, you will reap a bad response. Examples of this principle are all around us. This is not a coincidence! What goes around comes around.

The Word of God is life transforming. I know this for a fact. I have learned and loved the Bible, and I try to live like the Bible tells me to live. It has transformed my life.

> For the word of God is quick, and powerful, and sharper than any twoedged sword, piercing even to the dividing asunder of soul and spirit, and of the joints and marrow, and is a discerner of the thoughts and intents of the heart. Hebrews 4:12

The Bible addresses our feelings, emotions, intentions, and motives. I have experienced this transformation for more than forty-five years. And I have observed this transforming power in many others during my lifetime. The Word of God is the source for the transformation.

> I beseech you therefore, brethren, by the mercies of God, that ye present your bodies a living sacrifice, holy, acceptable unto God, which is your reasonable service. And be not conformed to this world: but be ye transformed by the renewing of your mind, that ye may prove what is that good, and acceptable, and perfect, will of God. Romans 12:1–2

I once heard someone share this thought and wrote it in the flyleaf of my Bible: "If God created man with a desire to know him, we would expect his message to have some unique properties:

- It would be widely distributed so man could attain it easily.
- It would be preserved through time without corruption.
- It would be completely accurate historically.
- It would not be prone to scientific error or false beliefs held by the people of that time.
- It would present true, unified answers to the difficult questions of life.

The Bible stands alone as the only religious text that can claim it meets all the above criteria.

Whenever I consider this issue, I think of an illustration I once heard. As one old-fashioned, Southern preacher stood holding his Bible in the air, he thundered out this message: "I believe this book from cover to cover! I even believe the line that says, 'Genuine Leather!'" He drove his point home.

The Bible is God's instruction manual for mankind and is the answer key to man's questions about life. His ways are clearly articulated and demonstrated in his Word. If one is to be reconciled to God and be in a healthy relationship with God, he must submit to God's way.

RECOGNIZING THE WORKS OF GOD

Santa Claus, the Easter Bunny, and Almighty God—what do these three have in common, one might ask. Many would answer, "They are all fictitious characters we never really see!"

How sad that people do not "see God." What if we did see him? Paul said of Jesus, "For in him dwelleth all the fulness of the Godhead bodily. And ye are complete in him, which is the head of all principality and power" (Colossians 2:9–10).

The Apostle John, authoring the book of Revelation on the Isle of Patmos, wrote:

> And I turned to see the voice that spake with me. And being turned, I saw seven golden candlesticks; And in the midst of the seven candlesticks one like unto the Son of man, clothed with a garment down to the foot, and girt about the paps with a golden girdle. His head and his hairs were white like wool, as white as snow; and his eyes were as a flame of fire; And his feet like unto fine brass, as if they burned in a furnace; and his voice as the sound of many waters. And he had in his right hand seven stars: and out of his mouth went a sharp twoedged sword: and his countenance was as the sun shineth in his strength. And when I saw him, I fell at his feet as dead. And he laid his right hand upon me, saying unto me, Fear not; I am the first and the last: I am he that liveth, and was dead; and, behold, I am alive for evermore, Amen; and have the keys of hell and of death. Revelation 1:12–18

Although we do not understand these physical visuals of God now, we can see what he has done and what he continues to do.

The Apostle Paul, as he was exhorting his fellow believers to serve, makes a very significant statement about this issue in Romans 15:4: "For whatsoever things were **written aforetime** were **written for our learning**, that we **through patience and comfort of the scriptures** might have hope." Let's take a deeper dive into what he is saying.

What was it in Paul's day that was "written aforetime"? It was the Old Testament Scripture. Paul was telling his audience that the Scriptures written so long ago were written for our learning today. What would we learn from the Scriptures? We would learn how God worked in the lives of men back then and that would teach us how God works in our life today. That would bring us hope. In other words, we could see God at work so that we could recognize how he was working today because he does not change. Through his work, we see him! He is really there!

I think a very significant thing to understand at this point is how important it is for us to be in the Bible on a regular basis. In our day and age, we have the great privilege of having the entire Bible. Paul and the believers in his day only had the Old Testament. Some of those in the Old Testament simply had a scroll or two or the words of the prophets of God who were sent to deliver the messages of God. It should be much easier for us to recognize the works of God today—if we are regularly in the Bible!

Recognizing the works of God is accomplished by connecting life's experiences with God's truth. We see his work every day, but our problem is that we don't ascribe the work to God. It takes a determinate effort to recognize that what you see is the work of God or God's handiwork. One needs to develop the habit of recognizing it and identifying it publicly and personally. This is such an important exercise in building a person's faith. Romans 10:17 tells us that "faith cometh by hearing, and hearing by the word of God." That is, when we connect our life experiences with God's truth, we recognize that the work is of God and that God is at work. This builds our trust and confidence in God. This helps us see him. He is no longer a fictitious character. He is real to us! He is a person! He is God!

Let's do a little thinking exercise to illustrate that truth. Did you know, **it will get dark tonight**. We absolutely believe this because we have seen it happen over and over! Do you ascribe this fact to being the works of God? The first chapter of the Bible teaches us this:

In the beginning God created the heaven and the earth. And the earth was without form, and void; and darkness was upon the face of the deep. And the Spirit of God moved upon the face of the waters.

And God said, Let there be light: and there was light. And God saw the light, that it was good: and **God divided the light from the darkness. And God called the light Day, and the darkness he**

called Night. And the evening and the morning were the first day. Genesis 1:1–5

Who was it that made light and darkness? Who made the morning and the evening to be the parts of the day? It was God.

Here is another question: If my friend Ron plants pumpkin seeds in his garden, what do you think will grow? Pumpkins! We absolutely believe this because we have seen it happen over and over. Would you ascribe this to the works of God? "And God said, Behold, I have given you every herb bearing seed, which is upon the face of all the earth, and every tree, in the which is the fruit of a tree yielding seed; to you it shall be for meat" (Genesis 1:29).

Let me give you one more example: January begins the foaling season here in the Bluegrass region of Kentucky. Pastures are filled with mares and foals. The scenes are charming and beautiful. This unique area in which I live encompasses several counties that are considered a giant equine nursery. Major breeds of the area include Thoroughbred, Standardbred, Saddlebred, Quarter Horse, Tennessee walking horses, and Mountain Horses. Understand this! **You never see a Thoroughbred mare give birth to an Angus calf!** She gives birth to either a cute little filly or a handsome colt! Would you ascribe this to the works of God?

And God said, Let the earth bring forth the living creature **after his kind**, cattle, and creeping thing, and beast of the earth **after his kind**: and it was so. And God made the beast of the earth **after his kind**, and cattle **after their kind**, and every thing that creepeth upon the earth **after his kind**: and God saw that it was good. Genesis 1:24–25

I think we have made the point. God is at work all the time, and that work is manifest all around us. We just do not recognize his work because we have not spent time in the Bible to learn this! When we see his work, he becomes real to us!

Now, you might be thinking, "**I've never looked at it like this before!**" That's right. That is where our failure happens. Because we are not immersed in the Word of God, the works of God are not so evident, and we fail to recognize them as God at work.

When you study the Bible, you realize that the people recorded therein needed to be constantly guided by God's Word. If not, they quickly went astray. It is no different for you and me.

The book of Judges demonstrates this truth as the people needed to be led back to God time and time again. When they forgot the works of God, they would forget God and would go their own way or do their own thing. Acts 7, Stephen's defense, is a great passage to see how important it is to identify God's work as over and over Stephen reminds his audience about the historical events in Israel and ascribing these works in this nation to God. And think of this, most of the psalms are contemplations and acknowledgments of the works of God in the lives of men.

Get in the Bible, and with circumspection, you will see more of God than you can even imagine. When he becomes real to you, you will begin to relate more to him. That relationship is what God intended for Adam, and it is what he intends for you.

"YE MUST BE BORN AGAIN"

Jesus made this emphatic statement to Nicodemus, a religious man and a ruler of the Jews (John 3:7). Unless a person is "born again," they will never see the kingdom of God or enter the kingdom of God. This is an absolute truth. If not born again, one cannot see the domain of God.

It is vitally important that a person settle this issue of "spiritual rebirth." Whenever I try to address someone about this issue, I like to begin with a couple of questions. My first question is **"Could I ask you a very personal question?"** Most often I am met with a reply that says, "Sure, what is it?" The person has now opened the door for me to ask the second question, which is **"If you found yourself at the gates of heaven today, and the Lord met you outside the gates and asked, 'Why should I let you in?' What would you tell him?"**

This is not a tricky question, rather it is a very significant question. Think about it for a moment! If you understood heaven to be a real place of eternal dwelling (it is) and you thought that hell was the alternative (it is), wouldn't you want to be sure you were going to be in heaven forever when your life on earth ended?

What would your answer be to the question, **"Why should I let you in?"** Take a moment to consider what your answer would be! Have you got your answer? Your answer reveals what you believe about your own soul and where it will dwell eternally. It also reveals what or whom you are trusting in to make it happen!

Now that you have answered the question, let's see if it lines up with what God says about the question!

THE INCIDENT

Let's begin by looking at **an incident** that occurred **a long time ago** during Israel's wilderness wandering (Numbers 21:5–9). In the context, the children of Israel were wandering in the wilderness, having rejected the promised land for fear of the circumstances there. As they wandered, their discontentment grew, and a man named Korah gathered a group of influencers to stir up the people against Moses, God's appointed leader of his chosen people. The Lord judged Korah severely, swallowing up the rebel leader and his close band of co-conspirators. They went down into the pit alive! Can you imagine a scene like this happening before your eyes? Terrifying! Then this happened:

> And the Lord spake unto Moses, saying, Get you up from among this congregation, that I may consume them as in a moment. And they fell upon their faces.

And Moses said unto Aaron, Take a censer, and put fire therein from off the altar, and put on incense, and go quickly unto the congregation, and make an atonement for them: for there is wrath gone out from the Lord; the plague is begun. And Aaron took as Moses commanded, and ran into the midst of the congregation; and, behold, the plague was begun among the people: and he put on incense, and made an atonement for the people. **And he stood between the dead and the living; and the plague was stayed.** Now they that died in the plague were fourteen thousand and seven hundred, beside them that died about the matter of Korah. And Aaron returned unto Moses unto the door of the tabernacle of the congregation: and the plague was stayed. Numbers 16:44–50

It is unlikely that we look at the sin of rebellion today as God looked on it then. God was highly offended by man's rebellion, and he responded in his wrath! God doesn't change! God hates sin!

Not long after witnessing the Korah incident, the children of Israel moved into the desert of Zin, near Kadesh. In Numbers 20, they began to complain, gripe, and challenge God's motive for his treatment of them and the conditions they experienced in daily life. Griping, or complaining, was an outward manifestation of the rebellion that was in the hearts of the people. This is amazing when you consider the severity of God's judgment they had witnessed.

In a miraculous act of grace, mercy, and love, God provides water from the rock at a place called Meribah. From Meribah, the children of Israel were on the move again and needed to pass through Edom, but Edom rejected them and sent them away. They journeyed then from Kadesh to Mt. Hor. There the Lord judged Aaron and took his life. Again, rebellion was at the heart of the issue. Another judgment the people saw.

Israel responded by asking God to defeat the Canaanite king, Arad, who had been attacking their nation and taking prisoners. Israel vowed to God that if he would win the battle for Israel, they would fight for the Lord. This happens at a place called Hormah. Once again, as the children of Israel journeyed past Edom, the people began to complain and rebel against God and his leader Moses, impugning God's motives for his people! Here is the Bible context of the incident we are considering:

> And the people spake against God, and against Moses, Wherefore have ye brought us up out of Egypt to die in the wilderness? for there is no bread, neither is there any water; and our soul loatheth this light bread. Numbers 21:5

At this point, the lack of gratitude for the deliverance they had experienced in leaving Egypt is expressed by calling into question God's motive. **This did not sit well with God!** He grew weary of their griping and complaining. And so, he took action.

> **And the Lord sent fiery serpents** among the people, and they bit the people; and much people of Israel died.
>
> Therefore the people came to Moses, and said, We have sinned, for we have spoken against the Lord, and against thee; pray unto the Lord, that he take away the serpents from us. And Moses prayed for the people.
>
> **And the Lord said unto Moses**, Make thee a fiery serpent, and set it upon a pole: and it shall come to pass, that every one that is bitten, **when he looketh upon it, shall live**. And Moses made a serpent of brass, and put it upon a pole, and it came to pass, that if a serpent had bitten any man, when he beheld the serpent of brass, he lived. Numbers 21:6–9

Think about this; here is **a rebellious people**— discontent, griping, and complaining about their circumstance. They were ungrateful and cynical, complaining that "life is hard!" (Sin does make life hard—ever since the rebellion of Adam and Eve in the garden of Eden). They also spoke against God and Moses, his chosen leader. The people had the mindset about their situation: "It's God's fault and Moses's fault." Blaming others is dangerous, and it's never a solution.

In Numbers 21:6, we see **a responsive Lord**. Poor Moses! He is stuck in the middle of the conflict now. The people came to him, begging for Moses to speak to God on their behalf. And so, he does. Then the Lord responds to Moses and says, "You tell them . . ." God gives Moses, the intercessor, the remedy for their sinful actions that caused this broken relationship. Look closely and carefully at the remedy because it is a "**faith solution**" to man's sin problem, which is also important for you and me today.

In verse 7, we find **a repentant people**. Repentance and confession are the keys that open the door to deliverance. Changing their thinking and acknowledging their sin, the people were genuinely seeking forgiveness! It did not take long for the people to have a change of mind. There was immediate judgment on the sin. The circumstance had turned from loathing some bread to fiery, deadly serpents that were aggressive and on the attack.

We can learn from this that there is always a consequence for sin! The people had sinned against God by rebelling against his appointed leader. They were ungrateful for God's provision. They complained and were constantly griping about their circumstances in life. This behavior was a sin against God and his will. The people were now saying, "We have sinned, please stop the judgment!" Repentance means one is willing to stop the behavior that brought the judgment.

In verse 8, we find **a remedy provided—LOOK AND LIVE**! Really? Look and live? That's it? Would it be that simple? Yes, God was providing a faith remedy. It was not some set religious good works or rituals that would save them. God did not make the path of reconciliation hard or nearly impossible. He loved these people! **All they needed to do was believe God and turn by faith to the remedy God provided,** looking and expecting to be saved.

Stop and think for a moment. God's mercy and grace are active here and should be obvious to us. He was holding back the judgment they deserved. That is mercy! Then he gave them what they did not deserve; that is grace. God enabled their reconciliation.

Next, in verse 9, we see a **righteous promise**. If any man would look at the brass serpent, he lived—just like God said he would! You can trust God and believe him! He never fails! Never, no, never fails!

This is what true saving faith is—taking God at his Word, acting accordingly, embracing, and doing what God said. One turns away from their sinful desire with an honest plea for God's salvation, and God saves them! They are saved by grace through faith! They look and live!

THE ILLUSTRATION

Now that we've seen the incident in the Old Testament, let's look at an **illustration that was given by Jesus to a religious man** in the New Testament:

> There was a man of the Pharisees, named Nicodemus, a ruler of the Jews: The same came to Jesus by night, and said unto him, Rabbi, we know that thou art a

teacher come from God: for no man can do these miracles that thou doest, except God be with him.

Jesus answered and said unto him, Verily, verily, I say unto thee, Except a man be **born again**, he cannot see the kingdom of God. [A definitive statement—no neutral position—it's a strait gate and narrow way.]

Nicodemus saith unto him, How can a man be born when he is old? can he enter the second time into his mother's womb, and be born?

Jesus answered, Verily, verily, I say unto thee, Except a man be born of water and of the Spirit, he cannot enter into the kingdom of God. [A definitive statement—no neutral.] That which is born of the flesh is flesh; and that which is born of the Spirit is spirit. Marvel not that I said unto thee, Ye **must** be born again. The wind bloweth where it listeth, and thou hearest the sound thereof, but canst not tell whence it cometh, and whither it goeth: so is every one that is born of the Spirit.

Nicodemus answered and said unto him, How can these things be? [He didn't know even though he was a teacher in the Jewish religion.]

Jesus answered and said unto him, Art thou a master of Israel, and knowest not these things? [This religious man, as a master, was a highly respected teacher of the law in Israel.] Verily, verily, I say unto thee, We speak that we do know, and testify that we have seen; and ye receive not our witness. If I have told you earthly things, and ye believe not, how shall ye believe, if I tell you of heavenly things? And no man hath ascended up to heaven, but he that came down from heaven, even the Son of man which is in heaven. **And as Moses lifted up the serpent in the wilderness, even so must the Son of man be lifted up**: That whosoever believeth in him should not perish, but have eternal life. For God so loved the world, that he gave his only begotten Son, that whosoever believeth in him should not perish, but have everlasting life. [Now the explanation.] For God sent not his Son into the world to condemn the world; but that the world through him might be saved.

He that believeth on him is not condemned: but he that believeth not is condemned already, because he hath not believed in the name of the only begotten Son of God. And this is the condemnation, that light is come into the world, and men loved darkness rather than light, because their deeds were evil. For every one that doeth evil hateth the light, neither cometh to the light, lest his deeds should be reproved. But he that doeth truth cometh to the light, that his deeds may be made manifest, that they are wrought in God. John 3:1–21

There is so much to unpack in this passage. First, it is important to recognize who Jesus is talking to. Jesus was speaking to a religious man, who had no apparent relationship with God. I believe we can find many in the world today in this same condition. He believed about God but didn't know him and trust him. There is an eternal difference between awareness and faith! We can say that he was religious but lost. Physically alive but spiritually dead!

Second, Nicodemus did not understand the concept of salvation by faith, which is God's way of reconciling man to himself. Religion is man's way of addressing his reconciliation issue, but it is the wrong way. Over centuries, religion had perverted truth, and Nicodemus was no exception—he embraced the religion! It is what Nicodemus was taught, and sadly, it is what he taught to others! This created generational error.

Religion is a ceremonial observance whereas God's salvation is reconciling a broken relationship. Man-made religions are organizational and demand conformity to their own standard. God-made relationships are personal and life transforming.

Compare Adam and Eve's relationship with God before the fall with what God restores man to after the final judgment. Here is what man is restored to: "And I heard a great voice out of heaven saying, Behold, the tabernacle of God is with men, and he will dwell with them, and they shall be his people, and God himself shall be with them, and be their God" (Revelation 21:3). The word *tabernacle* means

HE BELIEVED ABOUT GOD BUT DIDN'T KNOW HIM AND TRUST HIM.

"dwelling place," so this is talking about the dwelling place of God. Unlike in the garden, where God would visit with Adam and Eve, in this new "dwelling place," God will dwell *with* his people. The people shall be the people of God. God himself will be with them. And God will be their God.

In that one verse, we see five phrases about close fellowship between God and man—a relationship, not religion or ceremony! This is what God wanted for Adam and Eve too. He wanted to restore a broken relationship and bring them back into the paradise he had created for them so they could fellowship with God.

We can draw from this truth, the understanding of what is important to God, even today! It is a close, personal, intimate relationship with man, not religion!

To make this even clearer in our minds, consider the definition of eternal life Jesus gives us in the Bible.

Jesus spoke these words, with his eyes lifted to heaven: Father, the hour is come; glorify thy Son, that thy Son also may glorify thee: As thou hast given him power over all flesh, that he should give eternal life to as many as thou hast given him. And this is life eternal, that they might know thee the only true God, and Jesus Christ, whom thou hast sent. John 17:1–3

We were once separated from God by our sin and living in spiritual darkness, but we are now restored through Christ to a knowledgeable and living relationship with God. We are "born again." We begin to know him as a person, instead of practicing a ceremonial observance of a concept. This is what Jesus was telling Nicodemus.

When we get in his Word and observe the world around us, we begin to see who God is and how he is interacting with mankind. As you hear him in his Word and see him in the world, your faith will grow.

Here are a couple more passages that are very clear about our reconciliation to God:

> For by grace are ye saved through faith; and that not of yourselves: **it is the gift of God**: **Not of works**, lest any man should boast. Ephesians 2:8–9
>
> But after that the kindness and love of God our Saviour toward man appeared, **Not by works of righteousness which we have done**, but according to his mercy he saved us, by the washing of regeneration, and renewing of the Holy Ghost; Which he shed on us abundantly through Jesus Christ our Saviour; **That being justified by his grace**, we should be made heirs according to the hope of eternal life. Titus 3:4–7

PASSING FROM DEATH UNTO LIFE

The Bible teaches us that in this process of salvation, the Holy Spirit is active, making us alive in spirit once again. He "quickens" us, meaning to make alive. We are said to pass from spiritual death to spiritual life. We are "born again"!

John, in his Gospel, also wrote: "Verily, verily, I say unto you, He that heareth my word, and believeth on him that sent me, hath everlasting life, and shall not come into condemnation; **but is passed from death unto life**" (John 5:24). Later, in his epistle, he would say, "We know **that we have passed from death unto life**, because we love the brethren. He that loveth not his brother abideth in death" (1 John 3:14). Amazing, isn't it? We can be sure of our salvation because we are alive in Christ and we love others who love him. This is what happens in a transforming faith! As we understand this transformation, we gain assurance and confidence.

SECURE IN HIM

What a wonderful realization I had the day I put my faith in Christ. The sin burden was lifted, and a new hope entered my experience. It did not take long though before I began to wonder if I was still saved! How certain was I that I would ultimately make it to heaven? Once I am saved, how will I stay saved? I don't think these are uncommon questions. Many people struggle with the certainty that they have been saved from their sin and will no longer be judged according to their sin. It is an amazing truth! And for some, it is hard to wrap their mind around the concept because we do continue to commit sin.

There is much written in the Bible to quell the fears of any who are wrestling with this issue. Consider the following passages and comments.

One day a group of unbelieving Jews pressed Jesus on his claim to be the Christ. Here is how he responded:

> Jesus answered them, I told you, and ye believed not: the works that I do in my Father's name, they bear witness of me. But ye believe not, because ye are not of my sheep, as I said unto you. My sheep hear my voice, and I know them, and they follow me: And I give unto them eternal life; and they shall never perish, **neither shall any man pluck them out of my hand. My Father, which gave them me, is greater than all; and no man is able to pluck them out of my Father's hand.** I and my Father are one. John 10:25–30

He referred to those who received him as the Christ as "my sheep." They were secure in him. He had the power and authority to give them eternal life. The picture is that of the sheep being secure in the powerful hand of Jesus. And not only were they securely held in the hand of Jesus, the Son of God, they were secure in the hand of God, the Father who was reinforcing the hand of the Son. No one or nothing could remove them from their position in God. This is true for those who have believed!

As the Apostle Peter opened his first letter to believing Jews who were scattered from Jerusalem to many other locations, he made this powerful statement:

> Blessed be the God and Father of our Lord Jesus Christ, which according to his abundant mercy **hath begotten us again unto a lively hope** by the resurrection of Jesus Christ from the dead, To an inheritance incorruptible, and undefiled, and that fadeth not away, reserved in heaven for you, **Who are kept by the power of God** through faith unto salvation ready to be revealed in the last time.
> 1 Peter 1:3–5

There are several key points here. These believing Jews were saved from their sin by the mercy of God based on the resurrection of Jesus Christ. He was the atonement for which they had long waited. Their inheritance, eternal blessedness, was the present and future benefit of this salvation. It was "incorruptible, undefiled, and would never fade away." What did those words mean to them?

From *Strong's Concordance of the Bible*, we find the word *incorruptible* means "uncorrupted, not liable to corruption or decay, imperishable, immortal."[14] The word *undefiled* means "not defiled, unsoiled; free from that by which the nature of a thing is deformed and debased, or its force and vigour impaired."[15] And finally, the phrase "fadeth not away" means "perpetual . . . not fading away, unfading, perennial."[16] A person's salvation, given by God once, is settled forevermore! Salvation is preserved by God, not the person who was saved. Hallelujah! I am secure in an unfailing God.

To these three comforting words and thoughts, Peter adds another layer of hope and encouragement. He tells these saved Jews that their salvation is "reserved in heaven for you." This is an incredible thought. That little phrase means to be guarded like a fortress. A person's salvation is so precious and important to God, that it is guarded like a fortress in heaven.

Imagine with me, if you will, a person who is repenting of their sin and believing that Jesus died for them. They meet in person with God and ask God to save them on the basis of their repentance and belief. The person and God actually sign a written contract regarding the person's forgiveness of sin and guarantee of eternal salvation. First, the new believer signs the contract acknowledging his faith. He acknowledges that it is God, and God alone, who can provide the salvation he is seeking. The believer is also forsaking any other who claims to be able to offer this salvation. Then God, in his mercy and by his grace, signs the contract, guaranteeing the salvation promise will be fulfilled and resulting in that believer living forever in heaven with God. The person is saved by "faith."

Once the contract is signed by both parties, a copy of the contract is given to the believer, and God keeps the other copy for himself. God takes his copy and places it in the vault of heaven—in the fortress of heaven—guarded by the army and the angels of heaven so no human being or enemy of God can get to it. This binding contract for the person's salvation is secure! This is the picture Peter is giving.

That "faith" contract is guarded until the day of the believer's death. At death, when a believer's soul departs his body, the salvation process turns from being saved by faith, that is, believing without seeing, to being saved by sight as they enter the presence of God in heaven. Peter described that day as being "revealed in the last time." They are now eternally secure! They have arrived at their home! This is their eternal home where they will live everlasting life in the presence of God. What an incredible thought! My friend, if you have sincerely trusted Christ as your Savior, your eternal future is set! You will live forever in heaven with God.

PRINCIPLES, CONVICTIONS, AND STANDARDS

As we restore our relationship with God and rest in our security in him, there are three words that will help us greatly if we understand them. These words are *principles*, *convictions*, and *standards*. Let's briefly consider each one.

Principles—A fundamental or basic truth. God's truth never changes! The Bible is filled with timeless principles for you and me.

Conviction—A state of begin convinced of error or compelled to admit the truth. When we are convinced that a principle applies to us, we can say we have a conviction. We embrace the truth with confidence and commitment.

Standard—A structure built for or serving as a base or support. (Notice that in this definition you don't see negativity.) Standards are set to support our convictions and keep us from violating the principles of God, thus keeping us from sin. So here is an important truth to grasp: **Standards are not established in our lives in order to gain favor with God—they are meant to protect us from sinning against God.** Remember, our problems begin within, from the heart of man. We need protection from ourselves!

Listen to the instruction from the wisest man to ever live as he instructs his son.

> My son, attend to my words; incline thine ear unto my sayings. Let them not depart from thine eyes; keep them in the midst of thine heart. For they are life unto those that find them, and health to all their flesh. **Keep thy heart with all diligence; for out of it are the issues of life.** Put away from thee a froward mouth, and perverse lips put far from thee. Let thine eyes look right on, and let thine eyelids look straight before thee. Ponder the path of thy feet, and let all thy ways be established. Turn not to the right hand nor to the left: remove thy foot from evil. Proverbs 4:20–27

Having taught his son that wisdom, Solomon talks about protecting the heart in order to use that wisdom. He speaks of controlling his tongue, guarding his eyes, and limiting where he went. His son would need to establish personal standards to control his behavior in each of these areas.

Protect your heart—The condition of your heart when a life issue comes your way will determine your response to the issue. A godly heart in that moment evokes a godly response. An ungodly heart will evoke an ungodly response. And we already understand that you will have to live with the consequences of your response!

The point is that we need to establish standards that will help us fend off those temptations that will certainly come! Having been set free from the bondage of sin, my attitude about standards should not be negative: Instead of "I can't," it should be different like "I don't want to" or "I don't have to." I have liberty in Christ—the freedom to do what is RIGHT! In the flesh, we rebel against rules; in Christ, we can rejoice in standards!

If we are going to successfully steward our lives and our testimony for the Lord, we must be anchored in Bible truth, convinced of its influence in our lives. We must set up a structure to protect us from our own sinful nature, our sensual flesh, the cultural influences that come flying at us every day, and the devil. We need to develop personal standards.

> IN THE FLESH, WE REBEL AGAINST RULES; IN CHRIST, WE CAN REJOICE IN STANDARDS!

In developing and living standards aligned with the Word of God, we can live victoriously in our restored relationship with our Creator.

CHAPTER 7

MY LIFE'S HELPERS

I had to learn that life and life's needs were too much for me alone, so God, in his mercy and grace, provided helpers for me as I journey along the way. Although some of these helpers did not fulfill their God-given responsibilities, they were there, and God was the provider of them.

As a child, my helpers were my parents. They had the God-given responsibility to raise me in the nurture and admonition of the Lord (Ephesians 6:4). God provided for me a wife to complete me (Genesis 2:18). In the communities in which I have lived, God provided a pastor that was there to help me grow in the grace and knowledge of the Lord Jesus Christ[17] and a church, which is a body of believers, to encourage and support me (John 13:34–35). The church is to be of mutual benefit to all its members as they help each other grow in the grace and knowledge of the Lord Jesus.

These are some of the earthly helpers God has provided. However, there is another helper, a heavenly helper.

THE HEAVENLY HELPER

The Holy Spirit is a heavenly helper that God has provided for me. The moment I repented of my sin and put my faith and trust in the finished work of Christ, I was born again. The Holy Spirit of God "quickened" me, giving me a new birth—a spiritual birth—and a new relationship with God called eternal life: "For Christ also hath once suffered for sins, the just for the unjust, that he might bring us to God, being put to death in the flesh, **but quickened by the Spirit**" (1 Peter 3:18). I became spiritually alive, and the Holy Spirit of God assumed residency in my body.

The Holy Spirit has several responsibilities impacting me continually as I live out my life on earth. The following are some of his ministries in me:

SEALS MY SALVATION

His presence in me seals me (Ephesians 1:13). The Bible identifies the Holy Spirit as the "earnest of our inheritance" (Ephesians 1:14). This simply means he is God's guarantee now that my salvation will be full and complete when I am in heaven with him. The word *earnest* is often spoken of as a person putting "earnest money" down to demonstrate "good faith" in a real estate transaction. The presence of God's Holy Spirit in us is his "down payment" that shows his good faith and commitment to completing the transaction.

For we know that if our earthly house of this tabernacle were dissolved, we have a building of God, an house not made with hands, eternal in the heavens. For in this we groan, earnestly desiring to be clothed upon with our house which is from heaven: If so be that being clothed we shall not be found naked. For we that are in this tabernacle do groan, being burdened: not for that we would be unclothed, but clothed upon, that mortality might be swallowed up of life. Now he that hath wrought us for the selfsame thing is God, **who also hath given unto us the earnest of the Spirit**. 2 Corinthians 5:1–5

TEACHES ME THE WORD OF GOD

In my introduction to this book, I mentioned how I did not understand the Bible when I first started to read it. This passage helps explain why it was difficult for me. Here the Apostle Paul is writing to a group of believers in the church at Corinth. What he reveals here is quite profound!

An unregenerate person, one still lost in their sin, is considered "spiritually dead." He is identified in the passage as the "natural man." The Word of God seems like "foolishness" to him. Why? Because the Bible is understood, or discerned, on a "spiritual plane."

Once saved and indwelt with God's Holy Spirit, the Holy Spirit teaches my spirit, which is now alive in Christ (1 Corinthians 15:22), so I discern the instruction on this spiritual level. I begin to see things from God's perspective. I learn the mind of Christ! Look at the passage:

But as it is written, Eye hath not seen, nor ear heard, neither have entered into the heart of man, the things which God hath prepared for them that love him. **But God hath revealed them unto us by his Spirit**: for the Spirit searcheth all things, yea, the deep things of God. For what man knoweth the things of a man, save the spirit of man which is in him? even so the things of God knoweth no man, but the Spirit of God. **Now we have received, not the spirit of the world, but the spirit which is of God; that we might know the things that are freely given to us of God.**

Which things also we speak, not in the words which man's wisdom teacheth, but which the Holy Ghost teacheth; comparing spiritual things with spiritual. But the natural man receiveth not the things of the Spirit of God: for they are foolishness unto him: neither can he know them, **because they are spiritually discerned**. But he that is spiritual judgeth all things, yet he himself is judged of no man. For who hath known the mind of the Lord, that he may instruct him? but we have the mind of Christ. 1 Corinthians 2:9–16

One thing I have learned, which has been incredibly important to me, is that the Holy Spirit knows at just what level of maturity I am all the time. He will not try to teach me more than I am ready to take in and digest. Some people can only manage the "milk of the Word" while others are ready for "bread" or "meat." This truth is observable in our individual lives. For example, have you ever been reading through a passage of Scripture you have read before and then find yourself saying, "Hmm, I never saw that in there before!" This is the Holy Spirit taking you deeper into the heart and mind of God! He knew you were ready for more.

> Now the Lord is that Spirit: and where the Spirit of the Lord is, there is liberty. But we all, with open face beholding as in a glass the glory of the Lord, are changed into the same image from glory to glory, **even as by the Spirit of the Lord**. 2 Corinthians 3:17–18

The Holy Spirit plays a key role in my personal development and spiritual growth.

CONVINCES ME OF SIN, RIGHTEOUSNESS, AND JUDGMENT

Think about the importance of this verse: "Thy word have I hid in mine heart, that I might not sin against thee" (Psalm 119:11). We often teach our children the Bible, including memorizing Scripture, and this is why. When we put God's Word in our hearts, it provides the Holy Spirit with the resources he will use when we are in the midst of a temptation. Here is how the Apostle Paul explained this to the church in Corinth:

There hath no temptation taken you but such as is common to man: but **God is faithful, who will not suffer you to be tempted above that ye are able; but will with the temptation also make a way to escape**, that ye may be able to bear it. 1 Corinthians 10:13

As a believer faces a temptation to sin against God, which is a common occurrence, the faithfulness of God provides a way for man to resist the temptation. The Holy Spirit bringing this memorized Scripture to our minds at just the right moment is one way God makes this provision.

This makes me realize how important God's Word is in my life, how real the Holy Spirit is, and how intimately interested God is in me. This is what a personal relationship is like! This is what spiritual life looks like! My heavenly helper is looking out for me and helping me fulfill my purpose of glorifying God.

GUIDES ME

The Holy Spirit also guides my life. He helps me know what is right and what may be wrong. He helps me apply God's Word to my life circumstances. He reigns in my life with peace and confirms his leadership as I face issues and make choices. It seems to me that the Holy Spirit is in constant communication with my conscience.

Wherefore, my beloved, as ye have always obeyed, not as in my presence only, but now much more in my absence, work out your own salvation with fear and trembling. **For it is God which worketh in you both to will and to do of his good pleasure.** Philippians 2:12–13

WE CAN GRIEVE OR QUENCH THE HOLY SPIRIT

In Ephesians 4:17–32, the Apostle Paul teaches us about the process of change that God takes us through as he conforms the believer to the image of Christ. He explains the process as putting off the old man, being renewed in our minds, and then putting on the new things we are learning. (More on that process later.) Then he gives a list of behaviors that we should change to illustrate this process. Near the end of the list he says, "And grieve not the holy Spirit of God, whereby ye are sealed unto the day of redemption" (Ephesians 4:30). If we fail to cooperate with the Holy Spirit's work in our lives, ignoring the new ways we have learned, it grieves him. The word *grieve* means "to make sorrowful."[18] This has a direct effect on our relationship with the Holy Spirit.

The Apostle Paul writes something similar to the church at Thessalonica. He says, "Quench not the Spirit" (1 Thessalonians 5:19). The Apostle Paul makes this simple, direct statement to instruct the believers in the newly formed church in Thessalonica how to live in light of the soon coming of the Lord Jesus Christ. In a very real sense, this is what maintaining your own little garden in Eden should look like. Look at the issues and actions Paul mentions:

> Wherefore comfort yourselves together, and edify one another, even as also ye do.
>
> And we beseech you, brethren, to know them which labour among you, and are over you in the Lord, and admonish you; And to esteem them very highly in love for their work's sake. And be at peace among yourselves.
>
> Now we exhort you, brethren, warn them that are unruly, comfort the feebleminded, support the weak, be patient toward all men. See that none render evil for evil unto any man; but ever follow that which is good, both among yourselves, and to all men.
>
> Rejoice evermore. Pray without ceasing. In every thing give thanks: for this is the will of God in Christ Jesus concerning you.
>
> **Quench not the Spirit.** Despise not prophesyings. Prove all things; hold fast that which is good. Abstain from all appearance of evil.
>
> And the very God of peace sanctify you wholly; and I pray God your whole spirit and soul and body be preserved blameless unto the coming of our Lord Jesus Christ. Faithful is he that calleth you, who also will do it. 1 Thessalonians 5:11–24

Notice first, the importance of our "church family" relationship. We should draw comfort from the church as we edify or encourage each other. We are to love those in leadership roles and have great appreciation and respect for them. We should hold them in high regard.

Then the focus shifts to each other. Look at each of these actions as personal responsibilities and embrace them now: comforting each other, honoring our spiritual leaders, living peaceably, exhorting each other to right living, supporting those among us who are weak, being patient with each other, seeking what is good for each other, rejoicing, praying, giving thanks, staying faithful, fleeing sinful behaviors, and separating from evil.

What we can learn from these passages is that as we fulfill our responsibilities, the Holy Spirit is free to guide us. Be careful not to grieve or quench him as he works in us for our benefit and for God's glory. There are many acts of our will mentioned in this short passage. The Holy Spirit knows our responses to these exhortations. He sees us cooperating or rejecting his influence.

HELPERS OF OUR JOY

The Apostle Paul had to do some difficult ministry work with the church in Corinth. The culture in that city was wicked, and the religious climate was one of sensual pleasure and sexual impurity. In his first letter to this group of believers, Paul confronted sinful issues that were well-known in the city, but the church had failed to police itself. As a result, their testimony and witness were feckless. However, those who suffered from this apathy were the church members themselves.

In Paul's second letter to them, commending them for finally addressing their issues, Paul makes this statement:

> Moreover I call God for a record upon my soul, that to spare you I came not as yet unto Corinth. Not for that we have dominion over your faith, **but are helpers of your joy**; for by faith ye stand. 2 Corinthians 1:23–24

As a minister of the gospel, Paul, with the calling and authority of an apostle (an eye-witness of Jesus), was to be a "helper of your joy." He was not the "boss" of these people. He ministered truth to them with the hope of restoring them to a right relationship with the Lord, thus restoring joy in their lives. The Corinthian believers were personally responsible for their behavior and for their standing with God.

To further demonstrate Paul's occupation as a minister of God's Word, I found it helpful and thought it would be helpful to provide Paul's personal testimony of his work. For him, this is what dressing and keeping his little garden in Eden looked like. Here is what he shared with the churches of Galatia:

> But I certify you, brethren, that the gospel which was preached of me is not after man. For I neither received it of man, neither was I taught it, but by the revelation of Jesus Christ.

For ye have heard of my conversation in time past in the Jews' religion, how that beyond measure I persecuted the church of God, and wasted it: And profited in the Jews' religion above many my equals in mine own nation, being more exceedingly zealous of the traditions of my fathers.

But when it pleased God, who separated me from my mother's womb, and called me by his grace, To reveal his Son in me, that I might preach him among the heathen; immediately I conferred not with flesh and blood: Neither went I up to Jerusalem to them which were apostles before me; but I went into Arabia, and returned again unto Damascus.

Then after three years I went up to Jerusalem to see Peter, and abode with him fifteen days. But other of the apostles saw I none, save James the Lord's brother. Now the things which I write unto you, behold, before God, I lie not.

Afterwards I came into the regions of Syria and Cilicia; And was unknown by face unto the churches of Judaea which were in Christ: But they had heard only, That he which persecuted us in times past now preacheth the faith which once he destroyed. And they glorified God in me.

Then fourteen years after I went up again to Jerusalem with Barnabas, and took Titus with me also. And I went up by revelation, and communicated unto them that gospel which I preach among the Gentiles, but privately to them which were of reputation, lest by any means I should run, or had run, in vain. But neither Titus, who was with me, being a Greek, was compelled to be circumcised: And that because of false brethren unawares brought in, who came in privily to spy out our liberty which we have in Christ Jesus, that they might bring us into bondage: To whom we gave place by subjection, no, not for an hour; that the truth of the gospel might continue with you.

But of these who seemed to be somewhat, (whatsoever they were, it maketh no matter to me: God accepteth no man's person:) for they who seemed to be somewhat in conference added nothing to me: But contrariwise, when they saw that the gospel of the uncircumcision was committed unto me, as the gospel of the circumcision was unto Peter; (For he that wrought effectually in Peter to the apostleship of the circumcision, the same was mighty in me toward the Gentiles:) And when James, Cephas, and John, who seemed to be pillars, perceived the grace that was given unto me, they gave to me and Barnabas the right hands of fellowship; that we should go unto the heathen, and they unto the circumcision. Only they would that we should remember the poor; the same which I also was forward to do.

But when Peter was come to Antioch, I withstood him to the face, because he was to be blamed. For before that certain came from James, he did eat with the Gentiles: but when they were come, he withdrew and separated himself, fearing them which were of the circumcision. And the other Jews dissembled likewise with him; insomuch that Barnabas also was carried away with their dissimulation.

But when I saw that they walked not uprightly according to the truth of the gospel, I said unto Peter before them all, If thou, being a Jew, livest after the manner of Gentiles, and not as do the Jews, why compellest thou the Gentiles to live as do the Jews? We who are Jews by nature, and not sinners of the Gentiles, Knowing that a man is not justified by the works of the law, but by the faith of Jesus Christ, even we have believed in Jesus Christ, that we might be justified by the faith of Christ, and not by the works of the law: for by the works of the law shall no flesh be justified.

But if, while we seek to be justified by Christ, we ourselves also are found sinners, is therefore Christ the minister of sin? God forbid. For if I build again the things which I destroyed, I make myself a transgressor. For I through the law am dead to the law, that I might live unto God. I am crucified with Christ: nevertheless I live; yet not I, but Christ liveth in me: and the life which I now live in the flesh I live by the faith of the Son of God, who loved me, and gave himself for me. I do not frustrate the grace of God: for if righteousness come by the law, then Christ is dead in vain. Galatians 1:11–2:21

I think you would agree that he was a helper of their joy, and his work in the service of God was unique. Ours is as well. God has a unique role for each of us, our little gardens in Eden.

Our pastor is also a helper of our joy. The Great Shepherd has called him to be an undershepherd and oversee a flock of God's sheep (Ephesians 4). You should understand that your pastor has been given to you by God to help you. As you participate in this relationship, he fulfills his godly role, and you experience the joy of the Lord.

CHAPTER 8

THE DAILY MAINTENANCE
OF MY GARDEN

We can learn from our past, and we can look toward the future, but we must live today. Our Christian lives will be lived one day at a time. Jesus taught his first disciples this simple truth in his Sermon on the Mount:

> Therefore take no thought, saying, What shall we eat? or, What shall we drink? or, Wherewithal shall we be clothed? (For after all these things do the Gentiles seek:) for your heavenly Father knoweth that ye have need of all these things. But seek ye first the kingdom of God, and his righteousness; and all these things shall be added unto you. Take therefore no thought for the morrow: for the morrow shall take thought for the things of itself. Sufficient unto the day is the evil thereof. Matthew 6:31–34

God knows what we need for daily living. We are not to worry. Rather we need to prioritize our relationship with him and let him do his work in us and through us, trusting that he will care for us. Each day will have its own challenges and difficulties. We need to "trust and obey."

So that brings us to the issue of "daily maintenance," or our daily walk with the Lord. Here are some of the things I have learned that have been very helpful to me:

MAINTAINING A FAVORABLE ENVIRONMENT

If one were to look for a simple statement for a Christian's daily responsibility, I think it would be this: **"I need to maintain a favorable environment in my life for the Holy Spirit to do his work."**

I was "quickened by the Spirit" when I put my faith and trust in the finished work of Jesus to save my soul and reconcile me to God the Father. I was reborn spiritually. The Holy Spirit immediately assumed residence in my body, sealing my salvation and becoming the earnest, or guarantee, of my expectation and my private tutor in helping me learn the Word of God and understand the will of God. He helps me "discern" the Word of God and convinces and convicts me about my application of God's will in my life. He is the one who helps me with my spiritual discipline.

The Bible teaches me not to "grieve" or "quench" the Holy Spirit. That frustrates the enabling grace of God in my life, keeping me from fully benefiting from this grace in my life. The Holy Spirit does not leave me when I grieve or quench him; however, it is as though he steps back and waits until I repent and return to a submissive posture with the Lord.

By means of illustration, the following is a quotation from Ken Turner, founder and director of High Impact Ministries, Benson, IL, a ministry to incarcerated juvenile boys, regarding the impact of a daily walk with God:

A few days ago, in our weekly Bible study in Normal, IL, we did a deep study of Proverbs 15. We looked at the chapter through the filter of Spiritual Discipline. We identified character traits mentioned in Proverbs 15 and discussed the importance of being disciplined with the help of God's wisdom and the Holy Spirit in us. Things such as speech, attitude, conduct, emotions, gratitude, temper, laziness, wisdom, foolishness, plans, thoughts, money, and a heart to listen are all mentioned in the chapter.

One of the new teen guys in my Bible study said, **"I need this so much because I have grown up with absolutely zero discipline in my life."** He went on to talk about the disadvantages of living in an environment without discipline, structure, or framework. So many of these youth mention having no support at home including no father figure, a mom who struggles with addiction, and no structure at all.

How profound coming from a "babe in Christ." This encouraged me about the work of God in a needy life. And aren't we all needy? No matter how little or how much experience and exposure to God and his Word we have had in our lives, God takes us where we are at and then begins to build, or rebuild, us into what he wants us to be. This happens day by day! If the environment is favorable, growth happens.

PRINCIPLES ARE FOUNDATIONAL TRUTHS!

Living life by principle is important. It is what brings stability and consistency to our lives. God's Word is filled with principles that God established. Consider this definition of *principle* from American Heritage Dictionary:

a. A rule or standard, especially of good behavior: a man of principle.

b. The collectivity of moral or ethical standards or judgments: a decision based on principle rather than expediency.[19]

When one is "principle driven," their actions and reactions, based on their belief, are responses to the guidance the principle provides. This is why understanding Bible truth is so important! Bible principles serve as the foundation of the Christian's belief and, as such, drive their behavior. When we trust and obey them, our lives glorify God. Our "light shines" in a way that people who observe us form a right opinion about who the God we serve is and begin to understand what he is like.

Consider, for example, this exhortation from the Apostle Paul to Pastor Timothy:

> But you, O man of God, flee these things and **pursue righteousness**, **godliness**, **faith**, **love**, **patience**, **gentleness**. Fight the good fight of faith, lay hold on eternal life, to which you were also called and have confessed the good confession in the presence of many witnesses. 1 Timothy 6:11–12 (NKJV)

Timothy was to pursue these traits in his life and be disciplined to apply the principles:

- **Righteousness**—I will always do what is right!
- **Godliness** (piety)—I will act in such a manner that others see the attributes of God in me!
- **Faith**—I will trust God and take him at his Word and will act accordingly!
- **Love**—I will sacrifice myself for the benefit of others, putting God and others first in my life!
- **Patience**—I will cheerfully endure by waiting on the Lord!
- **Gentleness**—I will treat others gently with humility!

In a daily walk with God, one learns these life principles, and the Holy Spirit helps him understand what they mean, why they are important, and what they should look like in the person's context of life. This lays a solid, principled foundation for living. The Holy Spirit then helps with daily application of these issue. This is personal discipline.

WHAT DOES IT MEAN TO "WALK WITH THE LORD"

The Bible clearly states that Enoch walked with God and Noah walked with God. And if you are in church regularly, or under some regular Bible instruction, you hear the exhortation to walk with God too.

Walking with God means a person orders his life by the truth God has given. This means that one lives in "intentional obedience." There is purpose and order in how they live. It results in a "proactive" lifestyle, not simply reactive to the culture and its attractions and expectations. We are to simply trust God and obey him. We put to practice in our lives what we learn from God's Word.

This thought begs the question, "**How universal is the possibility of walking with God**?" Walking with God means that we order our life based on the knowledge of the truth to which we have been exposed. At various times in history, people had different amounts or various levels of understanding because of the amount of truth God had revealed to them. No matter the level of understanding a person has of God and his Word, they have an opportunity and obligation to obey God and trust God.

God tells us in Romans 1 that he has revealed himself to the whole world through his creation (Romans 1:20).

This revelation is to such a degree of importance that man is without excuse not to know him. His creation testifies of his existence and power. So those who have little or no Bible exposure were to trust and obey the truth that they had been taught about God.

On the other hand, those of us in our age who have extensive resources to study and learn the Word of God have more of God's Word in our understanding to trust and obey.

Walking with God is not just for those who can read or those who can study. It is also for the illiterate who have to be taught verbally and perhaps not taught much. But whatever they've been taught and whatever amount of light they have been exposed to, they need to trust and obey. God has instilled in every man's conscience a measure of truth. And the creation around man triggers that consciousness.

A good illustration I consider is from my life experience ministering to communities of Black people. The illustration comes from the Black culture during the slavery era in America. The exposure many of the slaves had to the Word was often minimal, and the teaching of it quite basic because many black folks could not read or read well. Yet many of them had a deep, abiding faith in Christ. This can be demonstrated by some of the music that they sang: the old negro spirituals. I love these songs, and when I think about it, what is so lovable to me is their simplicity. Songs like "Steal Away to Jesus," "Swing Low Sweet Chariot," "Deep River," or "Sweet Little Jesus Boy" come to mind. While the music was beautiful and spiritual, it was oftentimes rather simple and lacking theological depth. It did, however, demonstrate a great measure of trust and obedience. Many of these folks were strong in their faith and walked with God.

I saw firsthand a similar situation when I made a ministry trip into Russia and Ukraine during the early stages of perestroika and glasnost. Much of the population had been deprived access to God's Word for decades. The culture reflected this. However, we met many who, with the little understanding they possessed, loved and worshipped God. We met pastors who had vibrant ministries even though they only had small portions of the New Testament to study and preach from. These men walked with God.

Walking with God means we order our lives to live in the ways of God. It means that we discipline ourselves to live spiritually, trusting the Lord and obeying his Word. This is an intentional determination of our will.

In Genesis 5, we learn that Enoch walked with God:

And Enoch lived sixty and five years, and begat Methuselah: And **Enoch walked with God** after he begat Methuselah **three hundred years**, and begat sons and daughters: And all the days of Enoch were three hundred sixty and five years: And **Enoch walked with God**: and he was not; for God took him. Genesis 5:21–24

How much of God's Word did Enoch know? From where did he learn God's Word? Who taught him? Enoch is not one of the most prominent characters in the Bible, but what we know of him is very significant. We can see in the following passages some of this significance.

> By faith Enoch was translated that he should not see death; and was not found, because God had translated him: for before his translation he had this testimony, that he pleased God. Hebrews 11:5

Without passing through the portal of death, Enoch was taken by God from his life on earth to be with God in heaven. Enoch had been fulfilling the will of God, pleasing him. He was maintaining his little garden in Eden too.

> And Enoch also, the seventh from Adam, prophesied of these, saying, Behold, the Lord cometh with ten thousands of his saints, To execute judgment upon all, and to convince all that are ungodly among them of all their ungodly deeds which they have ungodly committed, and of all their hard speeches which ungodly sinners have spoken against him. Jude 1:14–15

This passage clearly teaches us that Enoch learned some things about the will of God as he speaks of the beginning of the millennial reign of Christ (Revelation 19 and 20), a prophecy of things to come, and the final judgment of all sinners from all ages. How could he have possible known of this incredible event that is in our future? Apparently, his heart and ear were keen to the voice of God. And in case you missed it in Genesis 5, he walked with God for 300 years!

In the following pages, we will take a brief look at many of the passages that tell us how we walk.

WALKING BY FAITH

Many of the New Testament epistles were written to help believers "walk in faith." To walk by faith means that we believe God in his ways, and in turn, we order our lives accordingly. Sometimes his ways do not seem to be in concert with what we think, and it is at those times that we must choose God's way over what we think. Sometimes we would feel better if we had evidence or we could see the way. And so, what Paul says in 2 Corinthians 5:7 is that we are to walk by faith not by sight. **We are to take God at his Word and act accordingly.** (This is my simple definition of faith.) Whenever I think of this simple definition of faith, I think of Abraham and the covenant God made with him. It reads:

> Now the Lord had said unto Abram, Get thee out of thy country, and from thy kindred, and from thy father's house, unto a land that I will shew thee: And I will make of thee a great nation, and I will bless thee, and make thy name great; and thou shalt be a blessing: And I will bless them that bless thee, and curse him that curseth thee: and in thee shall all families of the earth be blessed. Genesis 12:1–3

If God said to me what he said to Abraham, I probably would have responded to him with a series of questions. "Where is that land?" "What would the nation be?" "How will you build my reputation?" "What blessing should I expect?" Rather than simple, immediate obedience, I tend to want more information before making a commitment. To be honest, that would have been rather faithless on my part. I would be asking for proof or outcomes. I just need to trust God and follow him. You know, "Not my will, but thy will be done!"

Paul also writes to the believers in Colosse: "As ye have therefore received Christ Jesus the Lord, **so walk ye in him**: Rooted and built up in him, and **stablished in the faith**, as ye have been taught, abounding therein with thanksgiving" (Colossians 2:6–7).

Paul is saying that our daily experience would be one of being firmly, or surely, settled in our faith, which is based in God's Word. The words "rooted and built up" lead to being "established" in God's way. This speaks of a secure and stable life.

WALKING IN TRUTH

As he was nearing the end of his time on earth, reflecting on his life, and thinking about the influence he had on others, the Apostle John wrote this in his third epistle: "For I rejoiced greatly, when the brethren came and testified of the truth that is in thee, even as thou walkest in the truth.

I have no greater joy than to hear that my children walk in truth" (3 John 1:3–4).

It was thrilling for John to hear of those he had taught in the Word, who embraced the teaching and made application of it to their own lives. It validated the investment of time and energy he made in them.

While thinking about this statement one day, I saw the depth of meaning in the verse that offers so much hope and encouragement. John was saying that there was nothing this world had to offer that would provide joy like his faith relationship and influence with these disciples of Jesus Christ. His earthly work would have eternal impact! Just an incredible thought! For John, it was so fulfilling. He was fulfilled in God's purpose and happy for those who were walking with God.

The real challenge for you and me is on a daily basis, how much does God's Word influence our living? Is it our guidebook and set of standards for living? Is it our instruction manual for managing our relationships? Do we look to God's Word regularly for direction in fulfilling our responsibilities? When we see what we are doing wrong, will we let God have his way in changing us? When we learn of things we should be doing, are we ready to embrace the truth and implement the new behavior? This is what it means to "walk in truth."

WALK IN NEWNESS OF LIFE

The Apostle Paul wrote to the believers in Rome about the expectation of life changes that one should experience when they trusted Christ as Savior: "Therefore we are buried with him by baptism into death: that like as Christ was raised up from the dead by the glory of the Father, **even so we also should walk in newness of life**" (Romans 6:4). Their baptism was a confession of their commitment to Christ and an indication that the believer was ready to change whatever God knew needed changing. Their behavior going forward would demonstrate the transforming power of God in working to conform the people to the image of Christ.

Notice that Paul said, "We also should walk in newness of life." It would be our choice, and "we should" make the right choice. We have to decide to embrace God's ways after turning away from our old life and trusting Jesus Christ for our salvation. Baptism is an expression of submission to the Lord and a statement of commitment to follow him.

One of the devil's lies is convincing mankind that change is hard, and we tend not to like change. We even resist it. We adopt an "this is how I have always done it" mindset.

Even if we might admit we struggle with the process of change, we must also admit we like what God's intended change will be. We are being conformed to the image of Jesus!

The Apostle John spoke of following Christ's example: "He that saith he abideth in him ought himself also so **to walk, even as he walked**" (1 John 2:6). Jesus set the example of "the right ways of God." Because *walking* has the concept of ordering one's life in a particular way, there would be an intentionality to living a particular way. We'll explore in more depth the change God takes us through a little later in this book. For now, we should have the expectation that God has something better for us, and he is ready, willing, and able to help us on this journey. We just need to trust and follow him. Let change happen! In fact, expect change!

WALK IN THE SPIRIT

In my mind, I often boil the living of the Christian life down to keeping my life environment favorable for the Holy Spirit to do his work! We looked at this earlier in this writing. When the environment is right, the Holy Spirit will produce his fruit. "What fruit?" one might ask. "But the fruit of the Spirit is love, joy, peace, longsuffering, gentleness, goodness, faith, meekness, temperance: against such there is no law" (Galatians 5:22–23).

I think you would agree that if this fruit described our lives, we would be thrilled! It is so appealing that we try to conjure up these traits ourselves. But remember, this is the fruit of the Holy Spirit, not of our efforts. Living in a state of submission to God, doing the will of God, we benefit from the fruit that he produces.

The Apostle Paul wrote to the church at Ephesus: "For ye were sometimes darkness, but now are ye light in the Lord: walk as children of light: (For the fruit of the Spirit is in all goodness and righteousness and truth;) Proving what is acceptable unto the Lord" (Ephesians 5:8–10).

It is interesting to see how Paul says that these believers in Ephesus "were sometimes darkness." He does not say that they were "in darkness." They were part of the darkness.

And now they had become light. It wasn't just that they were simply walking in the light, they were the light. Is that not what Jesus taught his disciples in the Sermon on the Mount? In Matthew 5:14, Jesus said, "Ye *ARE* the light of the world" (emphasis added). As the light, the disciples were to live in such a way that the world around them who were observing how they lived would form a right opinion of who their God was. This is how they would glorify God. We, too, should be careful how we live because what others see in us helps them form an opinion about the God that we serve. It should be the desire of every Christian that the projected opinion be an accurate opinion.

When you think about it, understanding that we are light puts a positive pressure on the believer to live right. We are not living right to gain favor with God; rather, we are living right so that others see their own sinfulness and need of a Savior. In seeing the light, we are hopeful that they will turn to God in repentance for salvation. This is really what the fulfillment of our purpose looks like as we live out our lives on planet earth after we're saved.

It is the Holy Spirit who "quickened me," or injected life into my spiritual deadness, when I repented and trusted Jesus Christ to save me. It is the Holy Spirit that teaches me God's Word (1 Corinthians 2:9–16) and then helps me discern its meaning and application in my life. He guides me in all truth (John 16:13). As I cooperate with him and dress and keep my little garden in Eden, the environment stays favorable for the Holy Spirit to produce fruit in my life.

Here is how the Apostle Paul describes this Spirit-filled living:

> There is therefore now no condemnation to them which are in Christ Jesus, who **walk** not after the flesh, **but after the Spirit**. For the law of the Spirit of life in Christ Jesus hath made me free from the law of sin and death. For what the law could not do, in that it was weak through the flesh, God sending his own Son in the likeness of sinful flesh, and for sin, condemned sin in the flesh: That the righteousness of the law might be fulfilled in us, **who walk not after the flesh**, **but after the Spirit**. For they that are after the flesh do mind the things of the flesh; but they that are after the Spirit the things of the Spirit. For to be carnally minded is death; **but to be spiritually minded is life and peace**. Because the carnal mind is enmity against God: for it is not subject to the law of God, neither indeed can be. So then they that are in the flesh cannot please God. Romans 8:1–8

Daily living with the Word, by the Spirit, enabled by the grace of God, looking for God's leading, trusting, and obeying—this is what life in my little garden in Eden should look like.

Galatians 5 is one of the clearest passages of truth to explain and illustrate what it means to walk in the Spirit. My spirit connecting to the Holy Spirit to direct my life is spiritual living or being spiritual. This passage has been a tremendous help to me in my life:

> For, brethren, ye have been called unto liberty; only use not liberty for an occasion to the flesh, but by love serve one another. For all the law is fulfilled in one word, even in this; Thou shalt love thy neighbour as thyself. But if ye bite and devour one another, take heed that ye be not consumed one of another.
>
> This I say then, **Walk in the Spirit, and ye shall not fulfil the lust of the flesh**. For the flesh lusteth against the Spirit, and the Spirit against the flesh: **and these are contrary the one to the other: so that ye cannot do the things that ye would.** But if ye be led of the Spirit, ye are not under the law.
>
> Now the works of the flesh are manifest, which are these; Adultery, fornication, uncleanness, lasciviousness, idolatry, witchcraft, hatred, variance, emulations, wrath, strife, seditions, heresies, envyings, murders, drunkenness, revellings, and such like: of the which I tell you before, as I have also told you in time past, that they which do such things shall not inherit the kingdom of God.
>
> But the fruit of the Spirit is love, joy, peace, longsuffering, gentleness, goodness, faith, meekness, temperance: against such there is no law. And they that are Christ's have crucified the flesh with the affections and lusts. Galatians 5:13–24

The Apostle Paul has reminded these believers that they are no longer under the law, bound in a religion. Instead, they are in a living relationship with God and his people. Their salvation is secure, and the rest of God's plan for their lives will be unfolding before their very eyes. According to this passage, that plan involves serving God and others instead of just serving self. We naturally serve ourselves. It will take intentional choices to serve God and others.

What I want to point out in this passage is that each of us will make decisions about how we will live. There are two significant things that influence our choices—our flesh (controlled by appetites and senses) and our spirit (controlled by our relationship with God).

To "walk in the Spirit" means to purposely order (or choose to live) our life in submission to God's will and ways as we are guided by his Word and the Holy Spirit. The Holy Spirit now lives in us, is always present with us, teaches us what God's Word says and means, and points out both truth and error, both righteousness and sinfulness. He applies his eternal truth to our present-day circumstances. This is wisdom.

The other choice we can make is to be controlled by our flesh—our natural sinful desires and appetites (affections and lusts), appetites that God gave us and we have misused or perverted.

As you can see from the passage, we cannot have it both ways. The flesh and the Spirit are at war with each other, and you (that is, your will) are the prize for which they are contending! Who will control your life? Notice the end of verse 17. A person might want to do right, but in their own flesh (or strength), they cannot. That is frustrating! It's confusing! Depressing! But here is the issue, whoever is winning the battle for "you" will be evidenced by the fruit that is being produced. The flesh produces one thing, the Spirit something quite different.

So here is a good exercise for us. Let us understand what is produced, and that will help us yield to either the flesh or the Spirit.

What does the flesh produce? In bulleted form, the following (definitions from *Strong's Exhaustive Concordance*) is a simple understanding of each word that describes the fruit produced when the flesh controls us (in opposition to God and his Spirit). And please remember, this is not just a description of the age or culture in which we are living, this is eternal truth; it has been this way since the garden of Eden:

THE FLESH AND THE SPIRIT ARE AT WAR WITH EACH OTHER, AND YOU (THAT IS, YOUR WILL) ARE THE PRIZE FOR WHICH THEY ARE CONTENDING!

- **Adultery**—married person engaging in sexual activity with someone other than their spouse.[20]
- **Fornication**—*harlotry* (including *adultery* and *incest*)[21]; from the Greek word *porneia*, which we get our English word *pornography*.

- **Uncleanness**—*impurity* (the quality); physically or morally unclean; filthy-minded.[22]
- **Lasciviousness**—"wanton (acts or) manners, as filthy words, indecent bodily movements, unchaste handling of males and females, etc."[23]
- **Idolatry**—image worship;[24] covetousness (Colossians 3:5).
- **Witchcraft**—from the Greek word *pharmakeia*—*medication* ("pharmacy"), that is (by extension), *magic* (literal or figurative): sorcery, witchcraft.[25] This would include the misuse of medications to purposefully alter one's mind or mood—get high!
- **Hatred**—*hostility*; by implication, a reason for *opposition*: enmity, hatred.[26]
- **Variance**—a *quarrel*, that is, (by implication) *wrangling*: contention, debate, strife, variance.[27] To be at odds with somebody.
- **Emulations**—properly *heat*, that is, (figuratively) "zeal" (in a favorable sense, *ardor*; in an unfavorable one, *jealousy*, as of a husband [figuratively, of God], or an enemy, *malice*): emulation, envy (-ing), fervent mind, indignation, jealousy, zeal.[28]
- **Wrath**—*passion* (as if *breathing* hard): fierceness, indignation, wrath[29]—violent anger.
- **Strife**—properly *intrigue*, that is, (by implication) *faction*: contention(-ious), strife[30]—to be "cliquish."
- **Seditions**—*disunion*, that is, (figuratively) *dissension*: division, sedition[31]—revolution against government or authority.

- **Heresies**—properly a *choice*, that is, (specially) a *party* or (abstractly) *disunion*—heresy [which is the Greek word itself], sect.[32]—practically it is choosing to believe or teach a way that is contrary to God's way.

- **Envyings**—*ill will* (as *detraction*), that is, *jealousy* (*spite*): envy.[33]

- **Murders**—(to *slay*); *murder:* murder, + be slain with, slaughter.[34]

- **Drunkenness**—Apparently a primary word; an *intoxicant*, that is, (by implication) *intoxication*.[35]

- **Revelries**—A *carousal* (as if *letting loose*): reveling, rioting[36]—wild immoral partying.

- <u>**And such like**</u>—meaning "things of this nature."[37]

Although this is a lengthy list, this is not an exhaustive list. This list describes the life of people who do not know God and are still lost in their sin. (They will not inherit the kingdom of God.) A believer's life should not be characterized by these things as it would give observers a wrong impression of who God is and what his character and nature are like.

So what Paul is teaching us is that when any or all these things are present in our life, it is because we are being controlled by our sinful nature. We chose to yield control to the flesh.

Do you want this to be a description of your life? If not, be intentional. Order your life by God's Word so you live God's way. As you tend your little garden in Eden, the Holy Spirit will make it fruitful.

So what would the Holy Spirit produce if we lived constantly yielded to him?

- **Love**—*affection* or *benevolence*; specifically (plural) a *love-feast*: (feast of) charity, dear, love;[38] This kind of love sacrifices self for the benefit of the one being loved.

- **Joy**—*cheerfulness*, that is, calm *delight*: gladness, (be exceeding) joy(-ful, -fully, -fulness, -ous).[39]

- **Peace**—*peace* (literally or figuratively); by implication *prosperity*: one, peace, quietness, rest, + set at one again.[40]

- **Longsuffering**—*longanimity*, that is, (objectively) *forbearance* or (subjectively) *fortitude*: longsuffering, patience.[41] It means having a long fuse instead of a short fuse, one that quickly flies off the handle.

- **Gentleness**—*usefulness*, that is, moral *excellence* (in character or demeanor): good(-ness), kindness.[42]

- **Goodness**—*goodness*, that is, *virtue* or *beneficence*:[43] being beneficial to God and others.

- **Faith**—*persuasion*, that is, *credence*; moral *conviction* (of *religious* truth, or the truthfulness of God or a religious teacher), especially *reliance* upon Christ for salvation; abstractly, *constancy* in such profession; by extension, the system of religious (gospel) *truth* itself: assurance, belief, believe, faith, fidelity.[44]

- **Meekness**—*gentleness*; by implication, *humility*.[45]

- **Temperance**—*self-control* (especially *continence*): temperance.[46] *Strong in* a thing (*masterful*), that is, (figuratively and reflexively) *self-controlled* (in appetite, etc.): temperate.

These things are the fruit of the Spirit. They are what the Spirit produces when we are in a right relationship with him—when we are not grieving and quenching him. These are not things we can produce or concoct on our own. When we try to do so, we are simply being hypocritical or being an *actor* under an assumed character.

Notice how Paul states this: Those who are Christ's (have trusted Christ and are saved by grace through faith) have crucified the flesh (made a choice that had consequences— they put the flesh to death allowing it to have no influence).

So here is the deal. We can evaluate our own spiritual life by asking ourselves which list describes the reality of the life we are living. Which list would you choose to describe you and your everyday life? Which list would you like to be a description of your friends and close associates? Remember, we cannot choose items from each list to have present in our lives, we get them when we yield to the leadership of either the flesh or the Spirit. Which one, not which ones! If I choose the flesh, the works of the flesh will be manifest. If I choose to walk in the Spirit, the fruit of the Spirit will be present.

I share this with you in the same spirit that Moses had as he addressed for the final time, a nation that he led forty years. That was a long time of influencing a group of people! He set the truth before them and reminded them of the two choices they had, including the consequences or outcomes of their choice. And then he encouraged them to make the right choice:

See, I have set before thee this day life and good, and death and evil; In that I command thee this day to love the Lord thy God, to walk in his ways, and to keep his commandments and his statutes and his judgments, that thou mayest live and multiply: and the Lord thy God shall bless thee in the land whither thou goest to possess it. But if thine heart turn away, so that thou wilt not hear, but shalt be drawn away, and worship other gods, and serve them; I denounce unto you this day, that ye shall surely perish, and that ye shall not prolong your days upon the land, whither thou passest over Jordan to go to possess it. I call heaven and earth to record this day against you, **that I have set before you life and death, blessing and cursing: therefore choose life**, that both thou and thy seed may live: That thou mayest love the Lord thy God, and that thou mayest obey his voice, and that thou mayest cleave unto him: for he is thy life, and the length of thy days: that thou mayest dwell in the land which the Lord sware unto thy fathers, to Abraham, to Isaac, and to Jacob, to give them. Deuteronomy 30:15–20

The children of Israel had a history from which they could study and learn. They had God-ordained leadership that instructed them, and they had the prospect of God's blessing on their lives if they made right choices. They were also given the possible consequence of bad or wrong choices. They were well-informed! But they had to choose for themselves!

In Moses's impassioned appeal, he reminds them of their accountability in heaven and on earth. God would be taking note of the choices, and people on earth would be too. The choice would directly affect their own lives, and it would impact the lives of "their descendants," the generations of family that would follow them.

What this passage speaks to me about is putting to death the notion that "my decisions only affect me." Nothing could be further from the truth. Many are affected by the decisions I make. It is believing the devil's lie that "it only affects me" that often gives us the courage to go against what God says. Do not take the devil's bait!

Paul would make walking in the spirit clear with this simple statement: "If we live in the Spirit, let us also walk in the Spirit. Let us not be desirous of vain glory, provoking one another, envying one another" (Galatians 5:25–26). Since one is saved, they should live the saved life and benefit from all that comes with it. Avoid looking back or going back to the old life of bondage.

The concern every man should have for himself is first, am I saved, and second, am I walking in the Spirit?

WALK IN LOVE

The Apostle Paul said, "Be ye therefore followers of God, as dear children; **And walk in love, as Christ also hath loved us, and hath given himself for us** an offering and a sacrifice to God for a sweetsmelling savour" (Ephesians 5:1–2).

This is basically saying to "order your life by loving." In the primary sense, it means to obey the two great commandments—love God and love others. We are to choose and then discipline ourselves to be consistently loving God and others. Even if we are not in the mood or if we don't feel like it right now, we are to order our life in love.

Loving God and loving others are intentional prioritizations of our behavior. As we grow in the grace of God, we begin to look at the world through the eyes of Jesus. Everywhere he went, he saw people hurting and in need. They needed to be loved. As we mature, we become more observant and aware of the world around us too. If we are intentional, we will see needs everywhere just like Jesus did. This opens the door of opportunity to show love to others. And I think you would agree with me about this: The volume of opportunity eliminates any reason or excuse that would keep us from loving others.

If that seems like a sacrifice to you, IT IS! That's the point. You sacrifice yourself for the benefit of others. "Why?" you might ask. Because that is who God is, and it is what he has done for our benefit. Once again, let's be reminded of this great verse: "For God so loved the world, that he gave his only begotten Son, that whosoever believeth in him should not perish, but have everlasting life" (John 3:16).

The Apostle John wrote, "And this is love, that we walk after his commandments. This is the commandment, That, as ye have heard from the beginning, ye should walk in it" (2 John 1:6).

Stop and think about your experience this past week. Can you point out opportunities that you took in order to love others? To love God? How does that experience measure up with God's expectation of his children to love him and to love others? Hmmm . . . it would be beneficial to us if we would go through this little thought exercise frequently.

WALKING IN GOOD WORKS

Good works seems to be a confusing issue for many. The words themselves are not confusing, rather the purpose of the good works is what confuses people. Here is a passage of Scripture that should clear up the issue for some:

> For by grace are ye saved through faith; and that not of yourselves: it is the gift of God: **not of works**, lest any man should boast. **For we are his workmanship**, created in Christ Jesus unto good works, which God hath before ordained that **we should walk in them**. Ephesians 2:8–10

The Apostle Paul teaches us that man is not saved from the penalty of his sin by doing good deeds or good works.

No, it is the grace of God, through faith, which saves man. And to be sure the readers didn't miss the point, he clearly states that our salvation is not accomplished by us, including our good works. If we could save ourselves by doing good, Paul says we would run around bragging about it. Then we would be guilty of the sin of pride!

However, once saved, we are "created for good works." This means "for the purpose of" doing good works.[47] Good works is part of God's purpose in conforming us to the image of his dear Son.

To me, this is easy to understand when I frame it like this: I know and have acknowledged that I went astray as a sinner, failing to live God's way. When God saved me, he began to bring me back into "his ways." My life was being changed "into the image of God." In faith and obedience, I put to practice that which I was learning in the Bible. The Holy Spirit was helping me every step of the way. He knew what I needed at any time, or at any moment, and he helped me understand what God said and how he meant for me to apply his Word to my life's context.

It wasn't that I was trying to produce "good works" to impress God or gain more favor with him. He is the one at work on me. I am "his workmanship," and he wants my life to demonstrate that truth to an observing world. As people see me, in particular the good works I do, they glorify God (Matthew 5:16).

WALK IN WISDOM

Knowledge and wisdom are not the same thing. Knowledge can be gained by man through experience and study. Wisdom is a gift from God. "If any of you lack wisdom, let him ask of God, that giveth to all men liberally, and upbraideth not; and it shall be given him" (James 1:5). Wisdom is the ability to make application of biblical principle to your life context.

Once again, this is some of the work of the Holy Spirit when we are in a right relationship with him. He helps us "discern" God's Word and make application of it to our circumstances. (To expand on this thought, see 1 Corinthians 2:9–16.) This is part of maintaining our little garden in Eden. Keep the environment favorable for the Holy Spirit to work.

The Apostle Paul told the believers in Colosse to "walk in wisdom toward them that are without, redeeming the time" (Colossians 4:5). Paul, too, was pointing out how God's Word, when obeyed and applied, created a different behavior that was observable. He reminds the church at Colosse to "get with it" because time is short and the need is great. Be intentional about living for Christ so others can see him through the window of you!

King Solomon articulates the rewards of walking in wisdom to his son in Proverbs 3 by personifying wisdom. It is a lengthy chapter, but let me encourage you to read through this contemplatively, slowly, giving thoughts to each phrase and how it impacts you.

My son, **forget not my law**; but let thine heart keep my commandments: for length of days, and long life, and peace, shall they add to thee. **Let not mercy and truth forsake thee**: bind them about thy neck; write them upon the table of thine heart: so shalt thou find favour and good understanding in the sight of God and man. **Trust in the Lord with all thine heart; and lean not unto thine own understanding. In all thy ways acknowledge him**, and he shall direct thy paths. **Be not wise in thine own eyes: fear the Lord, and depart from evil.** It shall be health to thy navel, and marrow to thy bones. **Honour the Lord with thy substance, and with the firstfruits of all thine increase**: so shall thy barns be filled with plenty, and thy presses shall burst out with new wine. My son, **despise not the chastening of the Lord; neither be weary of his correction**: for whom the Lord loveth he correcteth; even as a father the son in whom he delighteth. Happy is the man that findeth WISDOM, and the man that getteth understanding. For the merchandise of it is better than the merchandise of silver, and the gain thereof than fine gold. . . . My son, **let not them depart from thine eyes: keep sound wisdom and discretion**: so shall they be life unto thy soul, and grace to thy neck. . . . **Be not afraid of sudden fear, neither of the desolation of the wicked, when it cometh.** For the Lord shall be thy confidence, and shall keep thy foot from being taken. **Withhold not good from them to whom it is due,** when it is in the power of thine hand to do it. **Say not unto thy neighbor, Go, and come again, and to morrow I will give;** when thou hast it by thee. **Devise not evil against thy neighbor**, seeing he dwelleth securely by thee. **Strive not with a man without cause**, if he have done thee no harm. **Envy thou not the oppressor, and choose none of his ways**. For the froward is abomination to the Lord, but his secret is with the righteous. The curse of the Lord is in the house of the wicked: but he blesseth the habitation of the just. Surely he scorneth the scorners: but he giveth grace unto the lowly. The wise shall inherit glory: but shame shall be the promotion of fools. Proverbs 3:1–35

Even as I read through this passage again, I am reminded how encouraging and appealing wisdom is. It brings comfort and confidence, setting my heart at ease. It provides balance and stability. It builds and strengthens my faith and resolve. Wisdom is an important element of life.

WALK WORTHY

Walk worthy! What a responsibility! What an opportunity!

Consider the Apostle Paul's letter to the newly formed church in Thessalonica. He had left their presence just a short time earlier and then wrote this letter to them.

Ye are witnesses, and God also, how holily and justly and unblameably we behaved ourselves among you that believe: as ye know how we exhorted and comforted and charged every one of you, as a father doth his children, that **ye would walk worthy of God**, who hath called you unto his kingdom and glory. 1 Thessalonians 2:10–12

This is a rich passage of instruction for us. Notice how the apostle behaved in their presence. He was setting an example for these new believers, encouraging, and testifying of God's work in his own life. We might say, like the passage projects, an ideal father/child relationship. Paul saw this as a responsibility before them and before God. The whole purpose of doing this was for God's glory and to advance God's kingdom—his program.

Paul takes us deeper into the heart of God in his letter to the church at Colosse, and he shows us what this walk looks like. He wrote:

For this cause we also, since the day we heard it, do not cease to pray for you, and to desire that ye might **be filled with the knowledge of his will** in all wisdom and spiritual understanding; that ye **might walk worthy of the Lord** unto all pleasing, **being fruitful in every good work**, **and increasing in the knowledge of God; strengthened with all might**, according to his glorious power, unto all patience and longsuffering with joyfulness; **giving thanks unto the Father**, which hath made us meet to be partakers of the inheritance of the saints in light: Who hath delivered us from the power of darkness, and hath translated us into the kingdom of his dear Son: in whom we have redemption through his blood, even the forgiveness of sins:

Who is the image of the invisible God, the firstborn of every creature: for by him were all things created, that are in heaven, and that are in earth, visible and invisible, whether they be thrones, or dominions, or principalities, or powers: all things were created by him, and for him: And he is before all things, and by him all things consist. And he is the head of the body, the church: who is the beginning, the firstborn from the dead; that in all things he might have the preeminence. Colossians 1:9–18

As I read that passage, it helps me understand a little better what God's intent for me as a believer looks like. This is certainly the "abundant life" Jesus spoke of in John 14.

Imagine this—knowing the will of God, applying it to my life circumstance, living it out and pleasing God, being fruitful in all that I do, and in doing so, knowing God better, growing stronger in faith, having patience, and being joyful, while having the spirit of gratitude about everything. How could anything be better than this? And to put the cherry on top, experiencing this abundant life, all for God's glory!

In Ephesians 4:1, Paul wrote, "I therefore, the prisoner of the Lord, beseech you that ye walk worthy of the vocation wherewith ye are called." This is **"the divine invitation to embrace salvation of God**."[48] What an incredible opportunity for "whosoever will." We can live in the King's domain.

WALK AND PLEASE GOD

Once again, what an opportunity. And I remind you it is an opportunity because you and I have a free will. You can choose whether or not you want to please God. You can see this in Paul's statement to the church at Thessalonica: "Furthermore then we beseech you, brethren, and exhort you by the Lord Jesus, that as ye have received of us **how ye ought to walk and to please God**, so ye would abound more and more" (1 Thessalonians 4:1). Paul was "urging and exhorting" them to make the right choice by ordering their lives in a way that would "please God."

Imagine the opportunity this gives us. We can do something to please the Lord—to bring pleasure to him. It is not some fantastic act of thinking or doing something spectacular. No, it is simply trusting and obeying him. They were to be serious about their personal relationship with God. Getting to know him and learning his will for their lives were at the heart of this exhortation. They were to "dress and keep" their little garden in Eden. Remember, Eden is the place of God's delight and God's pleasure, the perfect will of God.

WALK HONEST TOWARD THEM THAT ARE WITHOUT

In my thinking, this exhortation adds a layer of understanding about the personal walk I am to have with God. As Paul continues in this letter to the Thessalonian believers, he exhorts them to focus their energy and efforts on developing themselves. We might call this spiritual growth or personal growth. In doing so, they would be useful vessels in the hands of Almighty God. He writes:

> But as touching brotherly love ye need not that I write unto you: for ye yourselves are taught of God to love one another. And indeed ye do it toward all the brethren which are in all Macedonia: but we beseech you, brethren, that ye increase more and more; And that ye study to be quiet, and to do your own business [that which you know to be God's will for your life], and to work with your own hands, as we commanded you; that ye may walk honestly toward them that are without, and that ye may have lack of nothing. 1 Thessalonians 4:9–12

As these believers lived out their salvation, they were demonstrating brotherly love. They would be making an impact on the lost world around them. Paul identifies the lost world as being "outside." They were outside the family of God. They were still lost in their sin and in need of the Savior. And once again, this certainly helps us understand what it means to glorify God. Our life, lived God's way, projects an accurate opinion of the character of God into the minds of the observers, especially those who need the Savior we have. As "salt of the earth," our lives make the lost world thirsty for something, and as light, they see a glimmer of hope.

As if that blessing were not enough, there is another blessing in this passage. Have you ever really considered the relationship between our behavior and God's blessing on our lives? Just take a look at the last phrase in verse twelve: "And that ye may have lack of nothing."

Really? Yes, that is what it says. We would lack nothing! Now, hold on for a moment. Don't go out of your mind in exuberance and greed at this thought. The lacking nothing is from God's perspective, not from our selfish, greedy, green eyes of envy. God knows what we need, and he is able and willing to meet those needs. Oh, what a wonderful God we serve!

I think it is necessary to remind ourselves that not all believers will live this way all the time. I know I will fall short far too often, and you will too. Let's consider this admonition from Paul to the church at Philippi:

> Brethren, be followers together of me, and mark them which walk so as ye have us for an ensample. (For many walk, of whom I have told you often, and now tell you even weeping, that they are the enemies of the cross of Christ: whose end is destruction, whose

God is their belly, and whose glory is in their shame, who mind earthly things.) Philippians 3:17–19

Don't you think this truth was obvious to the believer in Philippi as they considered the lost people in their community? Likely so, but perhaps they did not look at some believers who lived ungodly in the same light. Those people were to me marked, meaning the believers were to "take heed." Many a carnal Christian has led others astray. There is constant pressure from the world's cultures and from our peers to conform to their ways instead of living God's ways. And if we are honest, we are all too vulnerable to that ungodly pressure. Our walk should demonstrate a good example of our salvation in Christ! It influences others.

WALKING IN THE LIGHT — A TEST OF OUR SALVATION

As we order our lives by God's Word, we experience the ways of God. This is what it means to walk in the light. We live in fellowship with God by hearing his Word and then obeying him with the application of the truth we learn to our own lives. As we do this, the Holy Spirit of God produces his fruit in us. Recognizing this work gives us confidence that we are one of his children; we might say "assurance of salvation." The Apostle John teaches us the following:

This then is the message which we have heard of him, and declare unto you, that God is light, and in him is no darkness at all. If we say that we have fellowship with him, and walk in darkness, we lie, and do not the truth: **But if we walk in the light, as he is in the light, we have fellowship one with another, and the blood of Jesus Christ his Son cleanseth us from all sin**. 1 John 1:5–7

Walking in the light, where there is no darkness, helps our spiritual vision and improves our understanding. "Then spake Jesus again unto them, saying, I am the light of the world: he that followeth me shall not walk in darkness, but shall have the light of life" (John 8:12).

The Apostle Paul helps us understand walking in the light as he exhorts the believers in Rome:

And that, knowing the time, that now it is high time to awake out of sleep: for now is our salvation nearer than when we believed. The night is far spent, the day is at hand: let us therefore cast off the works of darkness, and let us put on the armour of light. **Let us walk honestly**, as in the day; not in rioting and drunkenness, not in chambering and wantonness, not in strife and envying. But put ye on the Lord Jesus Christ, and make not provision for the flesh, to fulfil the lusts thereof. Romans 13:11–14

Paul is talking about practicing the presence of Jesus in our lives. Live like he is with you all the time because HE

IS! As we are living with the awareness of the presence of God in our lives, it will have a powerful influence. We will begin to look at the world around us as he sees it. The light exposes the realities of sinfulness and failure. Paul tells us we should live our lives as though we were fully exposed by the noonday sun. He addresses our public behavior, our private behavior, and the heart motives that propel us through life. This all gives us confidence that we are the children of God.

Paul addresses this issue with the Ephesian church as well. He writes:

> For ye were sometimes darkness, but now are ye light in the Lord: walk as children of light: (for the fruit of the Spirit is in all goodness and righteousness and truth;) proving what is acceptable unto the Lord. And have no fellowship with the unfruitful works of darkness, but rather reprove them. For it is a shame even to speak of those things which are done of them in secret. Ephesians 5:8–12

As we walk in the light, those who observe us begin to form a right opinion about the person and character of God. We walk as his children should walk, discerning and separate from ungodliness, which exposes them.

THE CONSEQUENCES OF WALKING DISORDERLY

We are certainly learning that how we live as Christians is of great importance. I have often heard people excuse their ungodly behavior by quoting 1 Samuel 16:7:

> But the Lord said unto Samuel, Look not on his countenance, or on the height of his stature; because I have refused him: for the Lord seeth not as man seeth; **for man looketh on the outward appearance, but the Lord looketh on the heart**.

This is often said with the implication that the outward appearance of man is of no significance or consequence. That is not what the Samuel is teaching here! Man can only see the outward, but God can see the inward as well. Jesus, in his Sermon on the Mount, taught that the outward appearance and behavior of a child of God would influence the observing world's opinions about God. The visible behavior of the believer DOES matter! The Apostle Paul wrote to the young believers in Thessalonica:

> Now we command you, brethren, in the name of our Lord Jesus Christ, **that ye withdraw yourselves from every brother that walketh disorderly, and not after the tradition which he received of us**. For yourselves know how ye ought to follow us: for we behaved not ourselves disorderly among

you; neither did we eat any man's bread for nought; but wrought with labour and travail night and day, that we might not be chargeable to any of you: not because we have not power, but to make ourselves an ensample unto you to follow us.

For even when we were with you, this we commanded you, that if any would not work, neither should he eat. **For we hear that there are some which walk among you disorderly**, working not at all, but are busybodies. Now them that are such we command and exhort by our Lord Jesus Christ, that with quietness they work, and eat their own bread. 2 Thessalonians 3:6–12

Clearly, the apostle was saying there was to be consequence for wrong behavior. He also spoke of those consequences as symptoms by which one could evaluate their own walk. "For ye are yet carnal: for whereas there is among you envying, and strife, and divisions, are ye not carnal, and walk as men?" (1 Corinthians 3:3).

The envy, strife, and division were an indicator that something was wrong with their heart. That inward condition manifests itself outwardly in their lives.

DON'T WALK LIKE A LOST PERSON

Ephesians 4 is one of my favorite chapters in the Bible. It is so rich with instruction for living today. After laying out some doctrinal truth, the Apostle Paul tells the readers about the purpose of the church that Jesus Christ is building. God has called some people to be in critical positions to build this church. These ministers of truth are to equip saved people for the work of building up the church. The believers are to grow to intellectual and spiritual maturity. This would influence the way they lived.

Then he exhorts the saved Gentiles in Ephesus to live differently than the "rest of the Gentiles" were living. Who are "the rest of the Gentiles"?

The rest of the Gentiles are the "lost" people of Ephesus. They are not saved by the grace of God through faith in Jesus Christ. They are still lost—dead in trespasses and sins. These lost people live differently than how the saved are to be living. Consider the phrases in the following passage that describes their "walk" or characterizes their lives:

This I say therefore, and testify in the Lord, that ye henceforth walk not as other Gentiles walk, **in the vanity of their mind, having the understanding darkened, being alienated from the life of God through the ignorance that is in them, because of the blindness of their heart**: who **being past feeling have given themselves over unto lasciviousness, to work all uncleanness with greediness**. Ephesians 4:17–19

This really is a heartbreaking description of those who are lost. It also describes those lost people we see every day of our life. It is an important practice to consider from these phrases, God's description of how lost people order their lives:

- *In the vanity (futility) of their mind*—They are "empty-minded" when it comes to the things of God—intellectually bankrupt of God's work and ways.
- *Having their understanding darkened*—With no light, they walk in spiritual darkness. Jesus taught us in John 3 that men love darkness because it conceals their sinful activity.
- *Being alienated from the life of God*—Lost people are not in the family of God. Contrary to what many believe and say, we are not all the children of God. **"In this the children of God are manifest, and the children of the devil**: whosoever doeth not righteousness is not of God, neither he that loveth not his brother" (1 John 3:10).
- *Through the ignorance that is in them*—This speaks of their moral blindness. They do not look at behaviors in the same way God does.
- *Because of the blindness of their heart*—They have rejected truth, and this rejection has hardened their hearts. They have little, or no, spiritual perception.
- *Who being past feeling*—The idea in this phrase is that they have "passed by or gone beyond" any sense of guilt of shame that sin brings into the human experience. This is such an important realization

because it provides explanation for much of the sinful behavior that is so repulsive to believers.

For example, how is it possible that a bartender continues to shove drink after drink across the bar to a person that he knows quite well and understands has a family at home that is in need? How can they keep giving that person drink after drink knowing he will have to make his way off the barstool, out to his car, and drive home through their community without causing destruction or even killing someone? How is it possible? Well, the bartender has "passed by" or "gone beyond" any sense of guilt or shame for what he's doing. It is just the way of life!

Or consider this example. How is it that a drug dealer can provide drugs to children who are in elementary school, knowing that it will bring some of them into the pit of hell through addiction and lead them to an early death? How is it possible? They have passed by or gone beyond the sense of shame or guilt that sin brings into the human experience.

- *Have given themselves over to lasciviousness*— They have surrendered their moral standing to the temptations of sin. They have an unbridled lust that leads to outrageous and shameless behavior. They participate in the most wicked behavior with an insatiable appetite.

- *To work all uncleanness with greediness*—They have given control to their sin natures. They have put themselves into bondage, believing the choice will be worth it all!

While I am not attempting to minimize these thoughts or to offer excuses, I do want you to understand that lost people can't help themselves! They are lost sinners shackled to the slave master of sin. They are hopelessly lost without the mercy and grace of God. There is an old saying that challenges believers about their behavior: "Your life may be the only Bible some will ever read."

WALK CIRCUMSPECTLY

The Apostle Paul exhorted the believers in Ephesus to live a consistent life making application of the God-given wisdom they had gleaned while studying truth. "See then that ye walk circumspectly, not as fools, but as wise, redeeming the time, because the days are evil" (Ephesians 5:15–16).

The definition of *circumspectly* is "to live carefully, circumspectly, deviating in no respect from the law of duty."[49]

Really consider this encouragement: We are to live carefully by paying attention to what is going on around us as we make our way through life. The attractions, distractions, and temptations seem to gang up on us at times. Other times, things seem to be going well and are rather peaceful. This challenge is telling us that no matter what the circumstances of life seem to be at the moment, be careful and be on guard. Stay faithful to the Word of God and order your life by obeying that still small voice of the Holy Spirit who is leading us and guiding us toward "the promised land."

As we leave this section about walking, I want to make this point perfectly clear in your mind: Walking with God and attending events about God are not the same thing! One is a relationship and the other is a religion! Tending your little garden in Eden is about relationship and responsibility, not religious ceremony.

PRAYING AND PRAYER

Volumes of books have been written on the subject of prayer. Perhaps one of the most prolific writers on the subject is E. M. Bounds, a minister from the late nineteenth century into the twentieth century. I read some of his books early in my Christian life and found them quite helpful. Another writer who made an impact on me was John R. Rice with his book titled, *Prayer: Asking and Receiving*.

I will shamefully admit that a disciplined prayer life has been one of my greatest challenges as a believer. To have a prescribed time, with extensive lists, and categorized days for ease of memory just seemed to complicate the issue for me. I don't, however, discount their value.

It seems to me that most prayer meetings at church focus on health issues and praying for the missionaries the church supports. While those things are good, they sometimes become a bit rote.

I have met many who have kept a "prayer journal" of special prayer requests, and then when the prayer request is answered, it is noted in the journal. That is certainly an encouraging, faith-building exercise. It can be used as a testimony or a personal encouragement at a later date.

I have taken to heart Paul's admonition to a group of young believers when he said, "Pray without ceasing" (1 Thessalonians 5:17). This is such a simple verse with a profound meaning and application.

Pray = to offer prayers to God, to supplicate, worship.[50]

Without ceasing = without intermission, incessantly, without ceasing.[51]

What this means to me is this, I am to stay in a constant state of prayer. It is like being in the same room with the Lord, and when I want to say something to him or I need to ask him something, I do it! Right then! I don't trust my failing memory to do it later. This kind of prayer comes directly from my heart. It makes my relationship more relatable! It is "continuous maintenance"!

Oh yes, I do participate in prayer meetings with others or offer thanksgiving before a meal, etc. To me, the key here is that I recognize my relationship with God, and I participate in it with conversation. Yes, I know he knows my heart, but the Bible teaches me he wants me to express those heart desires to him. He wants to hear from me.

One more thought here. I find that praying often helps me to think through issues and it helps me discern the will of God. It is common that as I am praying, my thoughts are directed a particular direction. No accident here! The Holy Spirit is helping me at that very moment.

TRUST AND OBEY

Faith and *obedience*—these two words should be the guiding principles of our life. I have turned away from believing or having confidence in anything other than what God has said. What he has said is revealed to me in his Word, the Bible. That is what repentance led me to. This principle of faith is the reason and motivation for my reading, studying, and meditating on the Word of God.

I have spent a lifetime battling sin and so have you. We tried to do our life our way! Our way never fulfilled the hopes and dreams we thought it offered. That is because my way and God's way are not the same. I often think that doing life "my way" was like rejecting the instructions that came in the box or even just failing to read them. Partway into my pursuit of assembly whatever it may have been I was assembling, I realized I had done something wrong, and now I needed to start over.

The best example of this that I can think of in my own life is one Christmas buying a make-believe kitchen for my two daughters. There were three pieces in the set: a refrigerator, a stove, and a sink. I knew my daughters would enjoy playing house and knew when we purchased it that it would require assembly. It said that right on the box! It came flat in a box.

Each piece was made of a pliable tin metal. At first glance, it looked like it would be an easy assembly. And so, without even looking at the directions, I began to put the pieces together, which required putting a tab on one piece through a slot on another and then bending the tab over. It looked easy and obvious. And I can tell you now, my faith was in my own ability to get it assembled!

Not too long into the process, I realized that I had left out a piece or had forgotten a step, and now, I had to unbend the tabs and pull the pieces apart. After doing this a few times, some of the tabs began to break off because I had bent them too much. This was really frustrating! Before long, I was looking for tape to complete my assembly. That Christmas morning was one of the most frustrating Christmases I can remember. It would have gone completely differently if I would have looked at the instruction sheet first.

Once I read the instructions, all I had to do was follow them. You know, obey! This is what our Christian life should look like—trust God and obey him.

SUMMARIZING DAILY MAINTENANCE

It may be that we have just scraped the surface of this issue of daily maintenance and walking with God. This is enough, however, for us to get the picture of God's will in this area. We all have much more to learn, but this understanding should set us in motion on the right path of God's desire for us. Our faith and obedience bring him pleasure!

CHAPTER 9

GARDENING TIPS

The Christian life is about continual growth and change. In this chapter, we will consider several issues that will find you during your journey to spiritual maturity.

CHRISTIAN LIBERTY

In this section, I want to address what I have found to be a great misconception—Christian liberty. Let's begin by looking at Paul's statement to the churches of Galatia: "Stand fast therefore in the liberty wherewith Christ hath made us free, and be not entangled again with the yoke of bondage" (Galatians 5:1). The liberty he writes of is freedom! The believers realized it when they trusted Christ for salvation. This liberty is an act accomplished completely, once and for all, and cannot be purchased again. The bondage of sin is permanently broken in the believer's life.

Paul also wrote of this liberty to the Corinthian church: "Now the Lord is that Spirit: and where the Spirit of the Lord is, there is liberty" (2 Corinthians 3:17). And where is that Spirit today? He indwells the believer!

Once we accept the premise that the shackles of sin have been broken, it produces a sense of joy and rejoicing. We have been set free! Paul said, "Rejoice in the Lord always: and again I say, Rejoice" (Philippians 4:4).

So consider this question: Are you a rejoicing Christian? Or are you, like many, living in bondage to a religion? Jesus Christ died to give us LIBERTY—freedom! Freedom from:

- The PENALTY of sin . . . death!
- The POWER of sin . . . a way of escape!
- The PRESENCE of sin . . . death and hell are defeated!

The Christian liberty we have now is not the freedom to do anything we want to do. It is the freedom to do what is right! Because we are no longer slaves to sin, we have a choice! Jesus Christ has broken the shackles of sin that had enslaved us to the lust of the flesh, the lust of the eyes, and the pride of life. Paul put it this way as he reminded Titus of his ministry responsibility:

> Put them in mind to be subject to principalities and powers, to obey magistrates, to be ready to every good work, to speak evil of no man, to be no brawlers, but gentle, shewing all meekness unto all men. For we ourselves also were sometimes foolish, disobedient, deceived, serving divers lusts and pleasures, living in

malice and envy, hateful, and hating one another. But after that the kindness and love of God our Saviour toward man appeared, not by works of righteousness which we have done, but according to his mercy he saved us, by the washing of regeneration, and renewing of the Holy Ghost; which he shed on us abundantly through Jesus Christ our Saviour; that being justified by his grace, we should be made heirs according to the hope of eternal life. Titus 3:1–7

But today many Christians live with a negative, defeated attitude! "I can't go there because I'm a Christian." "I can't do that because I'm a Christian." "I can't wear those because I'm a Christian." "I can't drink that because I'm a Christian." And it seems like their life communicates to the world around them that "we can't do anything because we're Christians!" To many Christians, it is as though they were <u>burdened under a heavy yolk of rules</u>. Too rigid! Too hard! That's because they don't understand Christian liberty.

Do you think it is possible, or even likely, that many lost folks reject Christ or refuse to let him into their lives because they see real Christians who can't bear the load of perceived "rules and restrictions," and thus, they get the wrong impression of Christianity? The unbelievers say to themselves, "I don't want that kind of life!"

Well, this is not a new problem. The Pharisees did the same thing! Consider the situation we learn of in Mark 7.

Then came together unto him the Pharisees, and certain of the scribes, which came from Jerusalem. And when they saw some of his disciples eat bread with defiled, that is to say, with unwashen, hands, they found fault. For the Pharisees, and all the Jews, except they wash their hands oft, eat not, holding the tradition of the elders. And when they come from the market, except they wash, they eat not. And many other things there be, which they have received to hold, as the washing of cups, and pots, brasen vessels, and of tables.

Then the Pharisees and scribes asked him, Why walk not thy disciples according to the tradition of the elders, but eat bread with unwashen hands?

He answered and said unto them, Well hath Esaias prophesied of you hypocrites, as it is written, This people honoureth me with their lips, but their heart is far from me. Howbeit in vain do they worship me, teaching for doctrines the commandments of men. For laying aside the commandment of God, ye hold the tradition of men, as the washing of pots and cups: and many other such like things ye do.

And he said unto them, Full well ye reject the commandment of God, that ye may keep your own tradition. For Moses said, Honour thy father and thy mother; and, Whoso curseth father or mother, let him die the death: But ye say, If a man shall say to his father or mother, It is Corban, that is to say, a gift, by whatsoever thou mightest be profited by me; he shall be free. And ye suffer him no more to do ought for his father or his mother; making the word of God of none effect through your tradition, which ye have delivered: and many such like things do ye. Mark 7:1–13

The Pharisees were concerned about their tradition. In this passage, they mention tradition twice, and the Lord rebukes them each time. The rebuke teaches us that it is possible to have outward conformity to religion without inwardly having a heart for God! That is religion without relationship!

The Pharisees thought the disciples defiled themselves because they did not wash their hands before eating. The Pharisees were attacking the spirituality of the disciples because they had a wrong understanding of standards. The result was "**making the Word of God of no effect**."

IT IS POSSIBLE TO HAVE OUTWARD CONFORMITY TO RELIGION WITHOUT INWARDLY HAVING A HEART FOR GOD! THAT IS RELIGION WITHOUT RELATIONSHIP!

This would be a good time to ask yourself two questions: "Does the Bible make a difference in my life?" and "Am I exalting tradition over truth?"

The Lord Jesus Christ rebuked the Pharisees and then taught them their real need! To help us understand what

Jesus is teaching, let's consider these basic truths from the Word of God:

- Genesis 8:21—"The imagination of man's heart is evil from his youth."
- Jeremiah 17:9—"The heart is deceitful above all things, and desperately wicked: who can know it?"
- 1 Chronicles 29:17—"I know also, my God, that thou triest the heart, and hast pleasure in uprightness [integrity]."
- Proverbs 23:7—"For as he thinketh in his heart, so is he." Attitude determines action (behavior).

These are Bible truths that will never change. They are forever settled in heaven. With this understanding, now notice how the Lord corrects the Pharisees' idea of defilement:

And when he had called all the people unto him, he said unto them, Hearken unto me every one of you, and understand: There is nothing from without a man, that entering into him can defile him: but the things which come out of him, those are they that defile the man. If any man have ears to hear, let him hear.

And when he was entered into the house from the people, his disciples asked him concerning the parable. And he saith unto them, Are ye so without understanding also? Do ye not perceive, that whatsoever thing from without entereth into the man, it cannot defile him; because it entereth not into his heart, but into the belly, and goeth out into the draught, purging all meats? And he said, That which cometh out of the man, that defileth the man. **For from within, out of the heart of men, proceed evil thoughts, adulteries, fornications, murders, thefts, covetousness, wickedness, deceit, lasciviousness, an evil eye, blasphemy, pride, foolishness: All these evil things come from within, and defile a man.** Mark 7:14–23

Jesus Christ is teaching his disciples that man's problem is from within! Sin begins with an attitude in our hearts and then manifests itself as an outward action.

To help us develop and maintain a right attitude about standards and recognize our need for them in our own lives, it is so important that we understand that Satan will use the things of this world, the weakness of our flesh, and his deceitful devices to trigger sin that is already in us. He baits us then springs the trap. Think of Paul's words, "For I know that in me (that is, in my flesh,) dwelleth no good thing: for to will is present with me, but how to perform that which is good I find not" (Romans 7:18).

Paul had no confidence in himself to do right! These words Paul writes are difficult for us to accept. We are not quick to admit that there is nothing good in us. We often have a much higher self-esteem than this! The truth is that our estimation of self is usually way off target. We are sinners by nature and sin willfully. We are woefully deceived in our pride. Standards are set to preempt the temptations we know will come.

Consider James's comments on temptation and sin:

> Let no man say when he is tempted, I am tempted of
> God: for God cannot be tempted with evil, neither
> tempteth he any man: But every man is tempted,
> when he is drawn away of his own lust, and enticed.
> Then when lust hath conceived, it bringeth forth
> sin: and sin, when it is finished, bringeth forth death.
> James 1:13–15

We are all weak and vulnerable! We all have an appetite for sin. Sin is attractive to our sinful nature. We need to have a defense predetermined for when the temptations come. When we allow the temptation to "conceive" (that is, to find a beginning point), it will bring forth sin. Not might! Will! Sin separates unbelievers from God, affects believers' fellowship with God, and makes us ineffective in fulfilling our purpose. The standards are there to prevent "conception."

"Conception" is often preceded by strategic temptation. Knowing that temptations will come, we need to build a strong defense that will help us protect our hearts. Here is our hope and our help: "There hath no temptation taken you but such as is common to man: but God is faithful, who will not suffer you to be tempted above that ye are able; but will with the temptation also make a way to escape, that ye may be able to bear it" (1 Corinthians 10:13). This is just an incredible statement! Let's break it down a little bit.

The temptation you face is not unique to you—every man is tempted! However, God is faithful, and he is present when the temptation comes to you! God will not allow you to be tempted beyond what you are able to bear. He always provides the way to escape so you can have victory over the temptation. I find that utterly amazing!

This means we have a choice to make when we face temptation. We are at liberty to say no! Will we give in to it or stand tall in the power of God? Paul knows the answer and encourages believers: "Know ye not, that to whom ye yield yourselves servants to obey, his servants ye are to whom ye obey; whether of sin unto death, or of obedience unto righteousness?" (Romans 6:16). It is your choice! And think of the help already provided to us: "Thy word have I hid in mine heart, that I might not sin against thee" (Psalm 119:11).

COMPARING YOURSELF TO OTHERS— UNWISE!

Have you ever felt unjustly criticized or unfairly scrutinized? Most people feel this way at some point in their life. It can be very discouraging and, if left unchecked, can completely sidetrack one from doing the will of God.

Being critical of others often comes from an unmet expectation the criticizer has of the one being criticized. It is as though the criticizer thinks they know what is best for the one they are criticizing. This is not just common in the general culture—it is also prevalent in the Christian culture, and that is a sad testimony.

Consider this statement by the Apostle Paul as he faced this issue: "For we dare not make ourselves of the number, or compare ourselves with some that commend themselves: but they measuring themselves by themselves, and comparing themselves among themselves, are not wise" (2 Corinthians 10:12). Paul was saying it was a foolish thing for one person to compare himself with another. Why would that be so? This does seem to be our tendency in life. Teenagers are impacted by this attitude under the banner of "peer pressure." We adults call it "keeping up with the Joneses." (Whoever they are!).

The issue of comparing ourselves among ourselves is worth looking at in the greater context of Paul's statement, and then we'll draw some practical application for us from the passage. Paul wrote:

Now I Paul myself beseech you by the meekness and gentleness of Christ, who in presence am base among you, but being absent am bold toward you: But I beseech you, that I may not be bold when I am present with that confidence, wherewith I think to be bold against some, which think of us as if we walked according to the flesh. For though we walk in the flesh, we do not war after the flesh: (For the weapons of our warfare are not carnal, but mighty through God to the pulling down of strong holds;) casting down imaginations, and every high thing that exalteth itself against the knowledge of God, and bringing into captivity every thought to the obedience of Christ; and having in a readiness to revenge all disobedience, when your obedience is fulfilled.

Do ye look on things after the outward appearance? if any man trust to himself that he is Christ's, let him of himself think this again, that, as he is Christ's, even so are we Christ's. **For though I should boast somewhat more of our authority, which the Lord hath given us for edification, and not for your destruction, I should not be ashamed**: That I may not seem as if I would terrify you by letters. For his letters, say they, are weighty and powerful; but his bodily presence is weak, and his speech contemptible. Let such an one think this, that, such as we are in word by letters when we are absent, such will we be also deed when we are present.

For we dare not make ourselves of the number, or compare ourselves with some that commend themselves: but they measuring themselves by themselves, and comparing themselves among themselves, are not wise. But we will not boast of things without our measure, **but according to the measure of the rule which God hath distributed to us, a measure to reach even unto you.** For we stretch not ourselves beyond our measure, as though we reached not unto you: for we are come as far as to you also in preaching the gospel of Christ: not boasting of things without our measure, that is, of other men's labours; but having hope, when your faith is increased, that we shall be enlarged by you according to our rule abundantly, to preach the gospel in the regions beyond you, and not to boast in another man's line of things made ready to our hand. 2 Corinthians 10:1–16

This is an interesting passage from several perspectives. Paul was being judged by some in the church at Corinth about his person and his ministry. They had opinions about Paul, his work, and particularly, his authority. Paul knew who he was, and he knew what God had called him to do and how God had equipped him to do it. We might say, he knew where his little garden in Eden was and what God expected him to do there.

He had to "cast down" the thoughts and opinions that would oppose him or distract him from doing the will of God. Paul knew that using others to measure his own life was not a wise practice. "Others" are not the standard God uses to measure us. So as a steward of God, Paul went about his work and, in defense of his ministry, taught a very important life principle, "**Be the best you can be, for the glory of God.**"

"OTHERS" ARE NOT THE STANDARD GOD USES TO MEASURE US.

Have you ever heard someone say they wanted to be "the best" at something? Maybe someone says, "I want to be the best dad in the world!" or "I want to be the greatest salesman in the company." Attitude makes a lot of difference in one's life. It can be a great motivator, but it can also set you up for failure and disappointment! Attitude will shape your actions, and it can either bring unnecessary stress or set you free from stress. Your attitude grows out of your understanding of your purpose and the agenda you are pursuing. For the believer, that is "the will of God." There is a fine line separating a positive effect and a negative effect when it comes to your attitude. Consider these contrasting mindsets and their effects and then apply them to your life.

YOUR ATTITUDE GROWS OUT OF YOUR UNDERSTANDING. FOR THE BELIEVER, THAT UNDERSTANDING IS "THE WILL OF GOD."

A Destructive Mindset: "I want to be the greatest <u>fill in the blank</u> in the world." This mindset may sound like a good goal, but realistically, it is a terrible goal because it:

- Puts unnecessary pressure on your life. (It is your mindset or attitude—your choice!)
- Looks for results that are beyond your control. (You cannot control what others do!)
- Offers staggering odds for failure. (You against everyone else in the world!)

A Constructive Mindset: "I want to be the best I can be for the Lord's sake."

- Narrows the field of competition to ONE. (Me!)

- Offers hope that success is within reach through obedience and faithfulness.

The Contrasting Effect of Each Mindset: Consider how different the outcomes are for each mindset.

A destructive mindset has the attitude: "I want to be the greatest_____!"

1. You will concentrate on **impressing others**. Your focus is on outward appearance. "What do I look like?"

2. Your standard of measure will be **other men**. "How am I doing compared to how you are doing?"

3. You will **compete** against others. The result will be division.

4. You will seek **acceptance** by others (recognition, praise, etc.). You will be self-centered.

5. Your failures (which are certain) will be **discouragements**.

6. You will **drive** people away from you.

A constructive mindset has the attitude: "I want to do my best for God's glory!"

1. You will concentrate on **developing** your gifts and talents. Your focus is on the inner man. "What am I?" People see Christ in you!

2. You will measure yourself against **God's standard and calling on your life**.

3. You will **cooperate** with others. The result will be unity.

4. You will seek God's **approval** which results in joy and peace. You will be Christ-centered.

5. Your failures will be **stepping stones** or building blocks.

6. You will **draw** people to Christ.

That old axiom "Attitude Determines Action" certainly holds true here! For example, if my goal is to be the best father, it should be the best father I can be, not necessarily the best father in the world, or community, etc. I will focus on learning the qualities and skills of being a father so I can fulfill my responsibilities as a father. I will spend my time and effort learning and applying what I have learned. Progress and success are likely to be the encouragements I need to keep moving forward with the spirit of continual improvement.

The journey each of us is on is unique. God has a purpose for us, his will, and a plan to accomplish that purpose. He has equipped us to fulfill that purpose. Our responsibility is to discover and do the will of God. That is why a personal relationship is so important. Spending time in God's Word and being sensitive to the leading of the Holy Spirit should be a great priority to us. What others think we should do is irrelevant in the big picture of life. Oh, their counsel may be helpful as valuable input, but understanding the will of God is between you and God, and that is what really counts. The psalmist put it this way, "The steps of a good man are ordered by the Lord: and he [the good man] delighteth [is pleased, desires, finds pleasure] in his way [journey]" (Psalm 37:23).

Be the best you that you can be, by the grace (enablement)

of God! Tend to your little garden in Eden and don't let the others in life keep you from doing what God placed you there to do.

UNDERSTANDING THE PROCESS OF CHANGE

In chapter 7, I mentioned we would consider the process of sanctification a little further, and so, we offer the following thoughts.

Inherent in the process of Christian growth is the need for change. Change is readily acknowledged to be very difficult for many people. The ancient proverb says, **"You can't teach an old dog new tricks**." Well, we are not dogs, and we are not learning tricks. We are cooperating with God in his radical transformation of our lives!

All of us have things that need to change, and that will be the case until we die. **God's plan for your life is much more than having you attend church services on Sundays! He wants to change our lives so the people we come in contact with see Christ in us.**

DISCOVERING THE NEED TO CHANGE

How do we know when change is needed? One comes to understand this need to change when they are confronted with truth that is contrary to their experience or practice. Sometimes change doesn't take place because there is no confrontation with truth. It is easy to continue on the wrong path of life if you don't know it is the wrong path.

In Jeremiah 22:21, as God pronounces judgment on Lebanon and a man named Coniah, he makes this statement: "I spake unto thee in thy prosperity; but thou saidst, I will not hear. **This hath been thy manner from thy youth**, that thou obeyedst not my voice." Coniah had a pattern, habit, and manner of living; he would not obey God. He willingly refused to listen to God. It had been a pattern since his youth, and it was a bad pattern. Coniah needed this confrontation by Jeremiah to provoke the needed change in his life. This is a very important truth or concept for us to embrace as well. **We need to be changed! Transformed!**

You might be thinking right now, "Well, I am happy with the way I am." That is not the issue. Is God happy with the way you are? The answer is, "No!" There are some changes that need to be made.

It is very likely that you have already established many habits and patterns in your life. Some are good; others are not so good. God wants to change the bad habits and patterns in our lives as he conforms us to the image of his Son. The bad habits are destructive. They bring ruin into our lives. **They grieve God and keep us from glorifying God**, which is God's purpose for us.

THE PROCESS OF CHANGE
FOR THE BELIEVER

As we consider this passage in Ephesians 4, we can see how God wants to change us for **our good** and **his glory**:

> But ye have not so learned Christ; if so be that ye have heard him, and have been taught by him, as the truth is in Jesus: that ye **put off** concerning the former conversation the old man, which is corrupt according to the deceitful lusts; and **be renewed** in the spirit of your mind; and that ye **put on** the new man, which after God is created in righteousness and true holiness. Ephesians 4:20–24

The process of change follows the simple outline we find in this passage: **"Put off. Be renewed. Put on."** (The same outline is also found in Colossians 3:8–14.) This is the method, or process, God has chosen to use for changing us.

God is quite serious about your life. He wants you to be a "vessel fit for the master's use" (2 Timothy 2:21). Radical change may need to be made. Consider the message Jesus was preaching to his disciples: "If thy right eye offend thee, pluck it out, and cast it from thee: for it is profitable for thee that one of thy members should perish, and not that thy whole body should be cast into hell" (Matthew 5:29). That certainly seems radical! However, what Jesus teaches us here is the importance of spiritual change in relationship compared to the well-being of our physical bodies. He wants us to be spiritually healthy and spiritually strong.

What behavior needs to change in your life? What pattern or habit of the "old you" needs changing? These are probing questions that make us uncomfortable for sure!

How is it that one discovers the change? King Solomon made a significant statement, twice! In Proverbs 14:12, he said, "There is a way which seemeth right unto a man, but the end thereof are the ways of death." Then, in Proverbs 16:25, he says, "There is a way that seemeth right unto a man, but the end thereof are the ways of death." Interesting! This exact repeat provides a double emphasis on this truth. It means we had better pay close attention to what he is saying.

When he speaks of a "way" he is speaking of one's journey or course of life. And so, we see that as this person is progressing down this path of life, they are doing so believing they are doing right or heading in the correct direction. They are sincere in their choice and in their confidence that this is a good thing. However, what that one does not realize is where the road of life is taking them. They lacked the knowledge or understanding of what is at the end of the road. If they know, they might change course.

So let's ask ourselves, "What does this person need?"

The answer is obvious. They need to be confronted with the truth or the reality of the danger that lies ahead. If they know before it is too late, they can decide to go a different way. In biblical terms, they can repent!

Now consider the Apostle Paul's statements in his letter to the believers in Rome:

> Now we know that what things soever the law saith, it saith to them who are under the law: that every mouth may be stopped, and all the world may become guilty before God. Therefore by the deeds of the law there shall no flesh be justified in his sight: **for by the law is the knowledge of sin**. Romans 3:19–20
>
> What shall we say then? Is the law sin? God forbid. Nay, I had not known sin, but by the law: **for I had not known lust, except the law had said, Thou shalt not covet**. Romans 7:7

As the law (God's Word) confronts us, we understand some behavior pleases God (we have conviction, or we are convinced it is right) and other behavior is sinful (we have conviction, we are convinced it is wrong). Sinful behavior offends God and condemns us. It leads to destruction and death, separation from God. It needs to change! The passage tells us that the bad, sinful behavior came because we gave in to our own lust, deceitful lusts (Ephesians 4:22). And don't miss this: we were the ones who were deceived! The promise or hope of pleasure and satisfaction was never delivered. Instead, we got pain and suffering. So deceitful is sin.

This is why it is important to listen to preaching, to be in a Bible-preaching church, and to read your Bible. As we are confronted by God's Word, the truth, we discover the need to change. The Word of God should have a constant presence and influence on our lives.

TAKE PERSONAL RESPONSIBILITY

Having discovered the need, the next step is to **take personal responsibility for your sin**. Once again, we look to King Solomon for some wisdom about this issue: "He that covereth his sins shall not prosper: but whoso confesseth and forsaketh them shall have mercy" (Proverbs 28:13). Wow, what a verse to test our real faith! If we believed the outcomes, not prospering compared to receiving mercy, we would be immediately confessing sin when we realized its presence. Confessing means we agree with God that the behavior is wrong; it is sinful. Forsaking is our determination to intentionally avoid repeating the behavior. This is the fruit of genuine repentance. Consider these words of confession from King David:

> Have mercy upon me, O God, according to thy lovingkindness: according unto the multitude of thy tender mercies blot out **my transgressions**. Wash me throughly from **mine iniquity**, and cleanse me from **my sin**. For I acknowledge **my transgressions**: and **my sin** is ever before me. Against thee, thee only, have **I sinned**, and done this evil in thy sight: that thou mightest be justified when thou speakest, and be clear when thou judgest. Psalm 51:1–4

David wasn't pulling punches in describing his sinfulness. He called it "transgression." This word means "a revolt (national, moral or religious):—rebellion, sin, transgression, trespass."[52] He saw his sin as being against God, his will, and his ways.

David also called this behavior "iniquity." It was "perversity, i.e. (moral) evil:—fault, iniquity, mischief, punishment (of iniquity), sin."[53] He agrees that he is responsible for turning away from God and his truth.

Finally, David calls this behavior "sin." This means "an offence (sometimes habitual sinfulness), and its penalty, occasion, sacrifice, or expiation; also (concretely) an offender:—punishment (of sin), purifying(-fication for sin), sin(-ner, offering)."[54] He failed to meet God's measure of righteousness.

When you are convicted by the truth you need to realize that **you have chosen to sin against God**! Instead of being honest with God and ourselves, we try to blame others (Adam blamed Eve, Eve blamed the devil, etc.). We try to blame our background, upbringing, environment, etc. declaring, "I'm a victim!"

No! When our behavior is wrong, we are not the victim, **we are the offender**! A sinner! And we are personally accountable for it:

The soul that sinneth, it shall die. The son shall not bear the iniquity of the father, neither shall the father bear the iniquity of the son: the righteousness of the righteous shall be upon him, and the wickedness of the wicked shall be upon him. Ezekiel 18:20

So then every one of us shall give account of himself to God. Romans 14:12

The bottom line is that God KNOWS the truth about us! Your sin is between you and God. "Neither is there any creature that is not manifest in his sight: but all things are naked and opened unto the eyes of him with whom we have to do" (Hebrews 4:13).

CONFESSION

We have discovered the need to change! We have acknowledged that we are the one responsible for our sin. Now we **confess our sin**: "If we confess our sins, he is faithful and just to forgive us our sins, and to cleanse us from all unrighteousness" (1 John 1:9).

To "confess" means "to say the same thing," that is, to agree with God that your behavior is wrong, just like he says it is. It is very important that we understand this definition. For many, confession may be considered an admission of wrongdoing or informing someone you have done wrong. While there is a sense of admission in biblical confession, there is not a sense of informing. We don't inform God that we have sinned. He already knows! Our admission is that we finally agree with God that the behavior is wrong.

Please allow me to share with you a personal example. For a number of years, I practiced the religion of Catholicism.

On either Friday evening or Saturday evening, I would go to "confession" at the church. This was preparatory to being able to take "holy communion" on Sunday. The "confessional," or confession booth, was located somewhere in the sanctuary. It consisted of three compartments. One on each side for a sinner about to offer confession, and the center compartment for the priest who would hear the confession. When it was my turn to confess, I would enter the confessional booth and kneel down facing the center compartment. When it was time for my confession, the priest would slide a small door open, leaving only a fine screen between him and me. I would begin by saying something like, "Bless me, Father, for I have sinned. My last confession was . . . (I would tell him when the last time I was in the confession booth, e.g., "two weeks ago")." Then, as I had been taught to do, I would tell him what sins I committed and how many times I committed them. For example, I might say: "I took the Lord's name in vain three times. I disobeyed my parents eleven times." And the list would go on and on. The dirty little secret, however, was that I was not being truthful. I didn't keep track of the sins or keep a running total of how many or how often I committed any one sin. I just informed the priest of some things I had done. If I didn't tell him, he would never know! Confession to God does not work like that! Once again, he already knows! We just need to agree with him.

Notice what happens when we confess our sins. **God forgives!** He is faithful! Every time we confess, he forgives!

Stop and think of the importance of that statement. God is so merciful and loving. That offers so much hope and encouragement. He is just; he has the right, the authority, and the power to forgive us. Consider how the psalmist understood this:

> The Lord is merciful and gracious, slow to anger, and plenteous in mercy. He will not always chide: neither will he keep his anger for ever. He hath not dealt with us after our sins; nor rewarded us according to our iniquities. For as the heaven is high above the earth, so great is his mercy toward them that fear him. As far as the east is from the west, so far hath he removed our transgressions from us. Like as a father pitieth his children, so the Lord pitieth them that fear him. For he knoweth our frame; he remembereth that we are dust. Psalm 103:8–14

Certainly, our heavenly Father loves us and wants what is best for us. He wants us to agree with him about what that "best for us" is.

And the Prophet Isaiah said, "Behold, for peace I had great bitterness: but thou hast in love to my soul delivered it from the pit of corruption: for thou hast cast all my sins behind thy back" (Isaiah 38:17). He has done the same with our sins! They are behind him, so they should be behind us. God's forgiveness means he will never bring it up again or hold it against us.

The Apostle Paul wrote to the Roman believers: "Even as David also describeth the blessedness of the man, unto whom God imputeth righteousness without works, saying, Blessed are they whose iniquities are forgiven, and whose sins are covered" (Romans 4:6–7). The blood of Jesus Christ has covered our sins so they are no longer visible. And then later in the same letter: "But God commendeth his love toward us, in that, while we were yet sinners, Christ died for us. Much more then, being now justified by his blood, we shall be saved from wrath through him" (Romans 5:8–9). The old hymn writer had it right when he penned, "What can wash away my sins? Nothing but the blood of Jesus."

And we can certainly rejoice in this declaration from God in Jeremiah, "For I will forgive their iniquity, and I will remember their sin no more" (Jeremiah 31:34). He does not remember it. So we should not dwell on it anymore either. In fact, it may be insulting to the grace of God if you choose to dwell on our past sin that God has forgiven.

We **ask** for forgiveness by faith; we need to **receive** forgiveness by faith. In our outline, the words "put off" means "cast off, lay apart (aside, down), put away."[55] We forsake the behavior God is teaching us is wrong because we now agree with him, and we have asked for forgiveness, and he has granted it!

THE MAKEOVER

Having "put off" the old man, our next choice (step) is to "be renewed in the spirit of our mind." To "be renewed" means "to renovate,"[56] like renovating an old house or having a makeover. It is God who is in the process of "renovating" our lives. He is the makeover artist. "For we are his workmanship, created in Christ Jesus unto good works, which God hath before ordained that we should walk in them" (Ephesians 2:10).

What does he want to renovate? It is "the spirit of your mind." The spirit is the rational soul, the vital principle, our mental disposition. He wants us to think differently, and he wants to "clear our conscience."

Our mind is our intellect—our understanding. God wants us to begin to look at things from his perspective or to see things as he see things. God's focus is on changing the way we think. That will change the way we live and the things we do. He is not looking for mere outward conformity to the rules of a religion! He wants us engaged in a relationship with him, and he will accomplish the changes in us that need to be made.

Our thinking has been greatly influenced by the society in which we live—in particular, the patterns of life and the philosophies for living we embrace. The Apostle Paul warns us, "Beware lest any man spoil you through philosophy and vain deceit, after the tradition of men, after the rudiments of the world, and not after Christ" (Colossians 2:8). The world we live in influences our thinking, and much of that thinking is not in-line with God's thinking. What are some of these influences?

Our Formal Education—What if our education was

not Bible-centered? What if it was contrary to the Word of God? Remember, "There is a way which seemeth right unto a man."

When what you learn in school conflicts with God's Word, what are you going to believe? For example, regarding the origin of man, schools teach evolution while God's Word teaches creation. Are you going to continue to believe the health teacher who tells you that you can have safe sex with a condom, or will you believe the God who says to remain pure, and that any sexual activity outside the bounds of marriage is sin, it is wrong, and there will be consequences? Which teaching will you embrace? One's education is a major influence for one's life.

Our Family Environment—What our parents taught us, whether good or bad, has great influence. What if they did not know the truth of God's Word? "There is a way which seemeth right unto a man." Or what if they lived in rebellion to the Word of God? (For example, think of parents who say to their daughter "Don't listen to those people at that church!" and later admit to their daughter that they themselves "used to go to church.") They will likely say something like "blood is thicker than water" in their attempt to have you follow family tradition, even though the contest is tradition against God's truth. Family ties have great influence.

Religions of the World—Humanism: Man-centered vs. God-centered. "There is a way which seemeth right unto a man." There are thousands of man-made, man-centered religions in the world. Every religion has its teachings or doctrines. Many tell you what you must do in order to please their god or to go to a place of eternal bliss. The Bible says it is not by man's works or righteousness that God saves him and reserves a home in heaven forever. Rather the sinner is saved by grace alone, through faith alone, in Christ alone that pays the sin debt and saves the sinner. Which one would a man choose, and why? Consider what Isaiah wrote:

> For my thoughts are not your thoughts, neither are your ways my ways, saith the Lord. For as the heavens are higher than the earth, so are my ways higher than your ways, and my thoughts than your thoughts. Isaiah 55:8–9

Now that we have discovered the need to change, and we have taken responsibility for our sin, we need to renew the spirit of our mind. We need to get our attitude and understanding changed. The change involves more than confession of sin. It also includes a desire and a willingness to change. Surrender your will that says, "I'm in charge of my life," to God's will that tells us he is in charge. His plan is much better than our plan. I'll do whatever God wants me to do, even if I have to change some things. This must be our attitude even before he tells us what to do. We need to commit our will to him.

Here are some examples from Scripture of what this change looks like:

> For they themselves shew of us what manner of entering in we had unto you, and how **ye turned to God from idols to serve the living and true God**. 1 Thessalonians 1:9
>
> I beseech you therefore, brethren, by the mercies of God, that ye present your bodies a living sacrifice, holy, acceptable unto God, which is your reasonable service. And be not conformed to this world: **but be ye transformed by the renewing of your mind**, that ye may prove what is that good, and acceptable, and perfect, will of God. Romans 12:1–2

Now that you are willing, that is, you want what God wants for your life, the next step is searching the Scripture to find out what that might be. God will reveal through his Word what needs to change and how to change it. We need to embrace God's Word as the truth that needs to direct my life. Consider this exhortation from the Apostle Paul to Pastor Timothy:

"All scripture is given by inspiration of God, and is profitable for doctrine, for reproof, for correction, for instruction in righteousness: that the man of God may be perfect, thoroughly furnished unto all good works" (2 Timothy 3:16–17). God's Word shows us what is wrong, how to fix it, and how to keep it fixed.

One might ask, "Why do we study the Word of God?" Let's answer this question at a practical level. We study the Bible to:

1. **Know God**—To understand his person and his character. Jesus Christ said, "Search the scriptures; for in them ye think ye have eternal life: and **they are they which testify of me**" (John 5:39). Again, in his great high priestly prayer, he stated, "And this is life eternal, **that they might know thee** the only true God, and Jesus Christ, whom thou hast sent" (John 17:3). Think about it! YOU CAN KNOW GOD!

   Consider this illustration: Lebron James is perhaps the most famous basketball player in America. Do you know Lebron James? Or do you just know about him? There is a difference! Well God wants you to know and experience him. He wants to be more than a figment of our imagination. He wants us to see him as a person. Consider this description:

   > And they sing the song of Moses the servant of God, and the song of the Lamb, saying, Great and marvellous are thy works, Lord God Almighty; just and true are thy ways, thou King of saints. Who shall not fear thee, O Lord, and glorify thy name? for thou only art holy: for all nations shall come and worship before thee; for thy judgments are made manifest. Revelation 15:3–4

This sounds like one who "knows God." Well, it is. This passage is speaking of the redeemed who are already in heaven with God. They are with him and know him.

2. **Know the Works of God**—Whenever I preach from an Old Testament passage, I begin by reminding the audience of this truth: "For whatsoever things were written aforetime **were written for our learning, that we through patience and comfort of the scriptures** might have hope" (Romans 15:4). Paul was writing to the believers in Rome and encouraging them. He told them they could look at how God worked in the lives of people in the Old Testament and that would teach them how God works today in their lives because God doesn't change. The same is true for you and me today!

Another passage that helps us understand the works of God is Paul's letter to the Corinthian church:

> Moreover, brethren, I would not that ye should be ignorant, how that all our fathers were under the cloud, and all passed through the sea; and were all baptized unto Moses in the cloud and in the sea; and did all eat the same spiritual meat; and did all drink the same spiritual drink: for they drank of that spiritual Rock that followed them: and that Rock was Christ. But with many

of them God was not well pleased: for they were overthrown in the wilderness.

Now **these things were our examples**, to the intent **we should not lust after evil things**, as they also lusted. **Neither be ye idolaters**, as were some of them; as it is written, The people sat down to eat and drink, and rose up to play. **Neither let us commit fornication**, as some of them committed, and fell in one day three and twenty thousand. **Neither let us tempt Christ**, as some of them also tempted, and were destroyed of serpents. **Neither murmur ye**, as some of them also murmured, and were destroyed of the destroyer. **Now all these things happened unto them for examples**: and they are written **for our admonition**, upon whom the ends of the world are come. 1 Corinthians 10:1–11

As we see things happening around us and connect it to the Word of God, it will build our faith in God. We will see how "real" he is. Paul said, "So then faith cometh by hearing, and hearing by the word of God" (Romans 10:17).

God is still working. He is working in the same way he has in the past. **He is working in your life.** "For it is God which worketh in you both to will and to do of his good pleasure" (Philippians 2:13).

3. **Know His Will for Our Lives**—The will of God is not as mysterious as some think it to be. Some think of it more as a "feeling" than "fact." God's will is found in God's Word. For example, consider these passages:

> **For this is the will of God**, even your sanctification, that ye should abstain from fornication: that every one of you should know how to possess his vessel in sanctification and honour; not in the lust of concupiscence, even as the Gentiles which know not God: that no man go beyond and defraud his brother in any matter: because that the Lord is the avenger of all such, as we also have forewarned you and testified. 1 Thessalonians 4:3–6
>
> In every thing give thanks: **for this is the will of God** in Christ Jesus concerning you. 1 Thessalonians 5:18

You might look at what is mentioned between 1 Thessalonians 4:3 and 5:18. Many things are written there that are obviously God's will for our lives. The will of God is much more than "Does God want me to be a missionary in Africa?" God has a plan for every part of your life. There are things to put off, to stop doing! There are things to put on, to start doing! Put off the old ways, the old man, which is corrupt. Be renewed in the "spirit of your mind." Let

God change you! Be willing to change! Search the Scripture, renew your mind. Study the Bible with purpose!

> Wherefore be ye not unwise, but understanding **what the will of the Lord is**. Ephesians 5:17

PUT ON THE NEW MAN

First, we considered "putting off the old man," which was corrupt according to deceitful lusts. Then we looked at "being renewed in the spirit of your mind." This was getting both our attitude and understanding renovated. Finally, we must "put on the new man." We are to live out the new life God is recreating in us. We are to make the changes that he deemed necessary and then consistently live according to his will, as we learned from his Word. Don't let your old manner of living play any part of your new life! We must practice what God is teaching us.

Our scriptural admonition is to change our ways once we are saved. We can look at this reality as both an opportunity and an expectation.

Living godly is an opportunity—"Then spake Jesus again unto them, saying, I am the light of the world: he that followeth me **shall not walk in darkness, but shall have the light of life**" (John 8:12). This is a very positive thought and a great opportunity for the believer! We have been set free from the bondage of sin and can now live free from its destructive influence.

Living godly is also an expectation—"Therefore we are

buried with him by baptism into death: that like as Christ was raised up from the dead by the glory of the Father, even so **we also should walk in newness of life**" (Romans 6:4). Once saved and surrendered to the Lordship of Christ, we should expect to be changing the way we live. Remember, "We are his workmanship, created in Christ Jesus unto good works, which God hath before ordained that we should walk in them" (Ephesians 2:10). God has a plan that he is executing in us and through us!

What we are learning through this process is the replacement principle. We are getting rid of some bad things and adding some good things as God is conforming us to the image of his dear Son. For example, here are some common things that might change:

Music—Getting rid of the bad music that appeals to your flesh and replacing it with good music that feeds your spirit. Some of your old music was promoting behavior that is contrary to God and his will, and that is what God is now changing. Trust and obey!

TV viewing—Getting rid of the bad television that was feeding your sinful flesh or corrupting your mind and replacing it with good programming or some other activity.

If you are not actively replacing the bad with good, in a moment of spiritual weakness, you'll fall back into the old patterns and habits.

There are three words I believe are key to helping us accomplish this renovation process: *obedience*, *motivation*, and *encouragement*.

Obedience—As we have learned what is right, what God wants us to do is OBEY. Obey means to listen attentively and then heed or conform to a command or authority. God is our authority; he does give us commands and expects us to obey them.

Obedience brings blessing: "Children, obey your parents in the Lord: for this is right. Honour thy father and mother; which is the first commandment with promise; that it may be well with thee, and thou mayest live long on the earth" (Ephesians 6:1–3).

Motivation—Think about this. We could be ushered into the presence of Jesus Christ at any moment. That could happen through the portal of death, or it could happen at the rapture of the church, which is the next major event on God's prophetic calendar. The Apostle Paul encouraged the Roman believers to live in a state of readiness for either scenario. He wrote,

And that, knowing the time, that now it is high time to awake out of sleep: for now is our salvation nearer than when we believed. The night is far spent, the day is at hand: let us therefore cast off the works of darkness, and let us put on the armour of light. Let us walk honestly, as in the day; not in rioting and drunkenness, not in chambering and wantonness, not in strife and envying. **But put ye on the Lord Jesus Christ**, and **make not provision for the flesh**, to fulfil the lusts thereof. Romans 13:11–14

Put on Christ—That is, practice the presence of Jesus Christ in your life. Imagine he is with you all the time, at every moment, in every place. How motivating would that be to commune with him and obey his commands? We don't have to just imagine—he is with us.

> Let your conversation be without covetousness; and be content with such things as ye have: for he hath said, **I will never leave thee, nor forsake thee**. So that we may boldly say, The Lord is my helper, and I will not fear what man shall do unto me. Hebrews 13:5–6

In his final command to his disciples, Jesus said, "Go ye therefore, and teach all nations, baptizing them in the name of the Father, and of the Son, and of the Holy Ghost: teaching them to observe all things whatsoever I have commanded you: **and, lo, I am with you always**, even unto the end of the world. Amen" (Matthew 28:19–20).

> And because ye are sons, God hath sent forth the Spirit of his Son into your hearts, crying, Abba, Father. Galatians 4:6

We need to **make a continual effort** to **realize the presence** of God. It is motivating! What will it do for us?

1. It will create a desire to do right—to please him. You have likely heard the old proverb, "When the cat's away, the mice will play." Well, when the cat is

present, things are different. When we understand and embrace the presence of Christ in our lives, things will be different than they used to be.

2. Practicing the presence of Christ will make us sensitive to sin, so we will confess it immediately. I remember hearing someone say, "Keep your sin account short." Unconfessed sin just hinders our spiritual life. Think of how you would respond if you had just taken the Lord's name in vain then immediately noticed he was standing right beside you. What would you say to him? I would say, "I am so sorry. What I just said was wrong!" His presence is what made me sensitive.

3. Practicing Christ's presence helps us to be instant in prayer. We are quick to communicate with him because we depend upon him. We don't want anything preventing him from helping us. If we recognized a need or had something to thank God for and Jesus were standing there beside you, wouldn't you just talk to him then?

4. When we realize he is with us, it makes us "Christ-minded." We see the world around us as he sees it. How we act and how we react would likely be different if we could see Jesus bodily in our presence.

5. And finally, practicing his presence helps us to see the needs of others. We move through life as though we were looking through his eyes, and we reach out to help those in need. Jesus did this, and if we knew he was right there with us, we would likely see what he sees.

Encouragement—The process of spiritual growth will have both success and failure. We can be encouraged when we recognize the successes. We must learn not to get "discouraged" when we fail. Failing is part of the process of change. Someone has said, "You cannot have victory if you do not play the game." In most athletic contests, you have a winner and a loser. However, both teams learn something. The Bible has something very clear to say about that: "For a just man falleth seven times, and riseth up again: but the wicked shall fall into mischief" (Proverbs 24:16).

I remember reading a wonderful book as a younger Christian that really was a help and blessing to me. It was titled *Bumps Are What You Climb On* by Warren Wiersbe. It encouraged me to use failures as stepping stones to success. When you think about it, resistance and obstacles are both used to build strength. Get up! Keep going! Try again!

Remember this, you will not arrive at perfection in this life, what is important is that you are headed in the right direction. Recognize your need of making changes, learn what and how God wants to change you, then cooperate with him, obey him, practice his presence, be encouraged, and don't quit. Put on the new man. You will reap the benefit of blessing, peace, and joy.

As one makes it a priority in their daily living to spend some time in God's Word, this simple practice becomes the "norm" for Christian living. As the Word of God convicts of sin, the surrendered Christian resolves to put away those behaviors. Exercising their will they intentionally discontinue the practice and eliminate the things that triggered or contributed to the sinfulness. They now understand the behavior is repulsive to God and harmful to their desire to live a life of purpose and joy.

SUFFERING AND CONSOLATION

We will experience suffering as we walk by faith in Christ. That is to be expected. We can also expect consolation to come from Christ as we do suffer.

> For as the sufferings of Christ abound in us, so our consolation also aboundeth by Christ. And whether we be afflicted, it is for your consolation and salvation, which is effectual in the enduring of the same sufferings which we also suffer: or whether we be comforted, it is for your consolation and salvation. And our hope of you is stedfast, knowing, that as ye are partakers of the sufferings, so shall ye be also of the consolation.
> 2 Corinthians 1:5–7

In verse 8 following this statement, Paul goes on to say that he was troubled beyond what he could bear, beyond his own ability and power, to the point of wanting to escape life itself! We were sinners condemned to death, Paul said, and God took care of that problem in saving us and delivering us from sin's wages, which is death. If God could do that, he would be able to comfort us no matter what the suffering might be.

Paul prefaced this testimony by saying, "Blessed be God, even the Father of our Lord Jesus Christ, the Father of mercies, and the God of all comfort" (2 Corinthians 1:3).

I have looked at suffering and consolation as part of our training to minister to others and to love others. When someone is going through a difficulty that we have gone through and we come alongside of them to comfort them, we are obeying God's command to love others. The sacrifice of love comes in being "uncomfortable" as we minister to them.

HARDEN NOT YOUR HEARTS

The writer of the book of Hebrews exhorted the reader with this warning:

> Wherefore (as the Holy Ghost saith, To day if ye will hear his voice, **harden not your hearts**, **as in the provocation**, in the day of temptation in the wilderness: When your fathers tempted me, proved me, and saw my works forty years. Wherefore I was grieved with that generation, and said, They do alway err in their heart; and they have not known my ways. So I sware in my wrath, They shall not enter into my rest.) Hebrews 3:7–11 (referring to Psalm 95:7–11)

The narrative of the day of provocation can be found in Numbers 14; and it is referenced in Deuteronomy 1:29 and following. The people were questioning God's motives and rejecting his leadership.

One thing we can certainly learn from these passages is that man will always react to the commands and leadership of God. He will either believe and receive, or he will rebel and reject. And when he rebels and rejects, his heart is hardened, or he becomes obstinate and stubborn toward the things of God. Once there is exposure to truth, there is no longer a neutral position toward any issue.

One of the ministries of the Holy Spirit, who lives in the believer, is to help us understand the heart of God from which the Word of God came. In other words, not only what it says but what it means. See all of 1 Corinthians 2. Paul came preaching the Word, but as it went forth, it did not go in Paul's wisdom but in the power of God (vs. 4) through the Holy Spirit. We get further insight into the process beginning in verse 9. Man can read words, but he cannot understand the intended meaning of them from God's heart unless the Holy Spirit instructs the man. And to be taught, the man's spirit must be alive! The truth is taught on a spiritual plane (vs. 13). And truth is understood on the spiritual plane! Before a person is saved, he is considered "dead" in trespasses and sin (see all of Ephesians 2)—in other words, spiritually dead. That is why he must be born again, quickened by the Holy Spirit!

The Holy Spirit knows just how much truth we can manage at any given point in time. He only teaches us what we are ready to receive (i.e., milk, bread, meat, etc.). I like to illustrate this by our own experience. Perhaps we are reading a passage we have read before and then something new comes out of it and we say to ourselves, "Hmm, I didn't see that in there before." The Holy Spirit knows you are ready to receive this because of your growth.

As he teaches us, we can receive truth or reject truth. Once learned, we are responsible to obey it (make application in our lives). See Ephesians 4:20–32 for the **wonderful, lifelong process** of changing us into the image of Christ, and then some examples of this: **Putting off the old man >> being renewed in the spirt of our minds** (attitude and understanding renovated) >> **putting on the new man** (the new things we are learning).

Hardening of the heart happens when we will not believe God or when we rebel against him. That is what the day of provocation spoken of in Hebrews and Psalm 95, narrated in Numbers 14, is showing us. God was not pleased with his people and their disobedience and rebellion, and he brought judgment to them.

When we begin to resist the Holy Spirit, we "grieve" him (Ephesians 4:30) and ultimately can "quench" him (1 Thessalonians 5:19). The process of spiritual learning and growth is interrupted, so to speak, until we repent and return. Then he gets back to work in us. The Holy Spirit knows our heart, and if we are not going to cooperate with him in the growth process, then he will stop the process until we get ready.

Adding more truth without having a willing spirit just hardens our hearts! We KNOW but refuse to DO!

CHAPTER 10

A FRUITFUL GARDEN

lmost every religion in the world emphasizes doing good works to gain favor with God in order to be saved from the penalty of their sin. How sad that so many are led astray by this man-centered teaching. A cursory study of the New Testament reveals to us that it is God who saves by grace through faith in the finished work of Jesus Christ.

Once a person is saved, the faith issue continues to be important. When we have the faith to trust him and obey him, he produces the fruit in our lives. Jesus clearly taught this to his followers:

> I am the true vine, and my Father is the husbandman. Every branch in me that beareth not fruit he taketh away: **and every branch that beareth fruit, he purgeth it, that it may bring forth more fruit**. Now ye are clean through the word which I

have spoken unto you. Abide in me, and I in you. As **the branch cannot bear fruit of itself**, except it abide in the vine; **no more can ye, except ye abide in me**.

I am the vine, ye are the branches: He that abideth in me, and I in him, the same bringeth forth much fruit: **for without me ye can do nothing**. If a man abide not in me, he is cast forth as a branch, and is withered; and men gather them, and cast them into the fire, and they are burned. If ye abide in me, and my words abide in you, ye shall ask what ye will, and it shall be done unto you. Herein is my Father glorified, that ye bear much fruit; so shall ye be my disciples. John 15:1–8

As we abide in Christ by tending our own little garden in Eden and doing the will of God, then God accomplishes his will through us. We have the privilege of sharing in the joy!

Sometime ago, I authored an article titled "Is God Looking for Accomplishment? Or Obedience?" The subtitle was "Doing Something Great for God! Really?" Let me share some of the thoughts from the article to help our understanding of what being "fruitful" means.

What is it that God needs or wants us to do for him? For some time now I have been troubled every time I hear someone talk about "doing something great for God." My natural inward response has been, "What could we possibly do 'for' God that he was not doing through us?" Jesus said in John 15:5, "I am the vine, ye are the branches: He that abideth in me, and I in him, the same bringeth forth much fruit: **for without me ye can do nothing**."

Under the inspiration of the Holy Spirit, Isaiah the prophet declared, "But we are all as an unclean thing, and all our righteousnesses are as filthy rags; and we all do fade as a leaf; and our iniquities, like the wind, have taken us away" (Isaiah 64:6).

The Apostle Paul reminded the church at Ephesus, "**For we are his workmanship**, created in Christ Jesus unto good works, which God hath before ordained **that we should walk in them**" (Ephesians 2:10).

He told the church at Philippi, **"For it is God which worketh in you both to will and to do of his good pleasure"** (Philippians 2:13).

And he wrote to the church at Thessalonica, "Wherefore also we pray always for you, that our God would count you worthy of this calling, and **fulfil all the good pleasure of his goodness, and the work of faith with power**: That the name of our Lord Jesus Christ may be glorified in you, and ye in him, according to the grace of our God and the Lord Jesus Christ" (2 Thessalonians 1:11–12).

And then preaching to the men of Athens at the Council of Areopagus that met on Mars Hill, Paul declared, "God that made the world and all things therein, seeing that he is Lord of heaven and earth, dwelleth not in temples made with hands; Neither is worshipped with men's hands, **as**

though he needed any thing, seeing he giveth to all life, and breath, and all things" (Acts 17:24–25).

Many a time, I have heard preachers use this famous quote by **William Carey**, "Expect great things from God. Attempt great things for God." The quote is often used in the context of doing something to build up a ministry. **I wonder how this quote would have played in the garden of Eden pre-fall.**

In the garden that God created and provided for its sustainment, Adam was placed there to "dress" (meaning to till it) and "keep" (meaning to tend to, guard, or watch over) it (Genesis 2:15). Adam simply needed to obey God and, in doing so, would fulfill his purpose there and bring glory to God. He was not expected to "do great things for God." **It was God who was doing the great things!** Adam was to obey. In my opinion, many believers are confused about this concept.

James, in this classic passage, warns against the mindset of doing something outside of the will of God, as if one were doing something of their own agenda, even if it was "for" God. He wrote:

> Go to now, ye that say, To day or to morrow we will go into such a city, and continue there a year, and buy and sell, and get gain: whereas ye know not what shall be on the morrow. For what is your life? It is even a vapour, that appeareth for a little time, and then vanisheth away. **For that ye ought to say, If the**

Lord will, we shall live, and do this, or that. But now ye rejoice in your boastings: **all such rejoicing is evil.** James 4:13–16

James rebukes the accomplishment motive and exalts obedience.

We could not find verses in the Bible where man does something "for God" and gains a more favorable standing because of it. **God is looking for obedience from us, not accomplishment!** Obedience is what pleases him. He wants us to learn and do his will (as part of his plan). Our will is what often gets in the way! In 1 Corinthians 6:19–20, we read, "What? know ye not that your body is the temple of the Holy Ghost which is in you, which ye have of God, **and ye are not your own?** For **ye are bought with a price**: therefore glorify God in your body, and in your spirit, **which are God's.**" The appropriate response for any who are subject to authority or leadership is "submission," and that is what God wants from us. It is the spirit of "not my will, but thy will be done."

OUR WILL IS WHAT OFTEN GETS IN THE WAY!

In Daniel 11, the word *exploits* is used twice in the KJV. However, it is not a word from the original text. The idea of doing *exploits* in this context simply means they "executed" or "performed" their vows. It does not mean they determined to do some fantastic, amazing, glorious thing that would impress God!

The following are uses of *obedience* in the Bible that clearly teach us what God's desire for us is:

- "By whom we have received grace and apostleship, **for obedience to the faith among all nations**, for his name" (Romans 1:5).

- "For as by one man's disobedience many were made sinners, **so by the obedience of one** shall many be made righteous" (Romans 5:19).

- "Know ye not, that to whom ye yield yourselves servants to obey, his servants ye are to whom ye obey; whether of sin unto death, or **of obedience unto righteousness**?" (Romans 6:16).

- "For your **obedience is come abroad unto all men**. I am glad therefore on your behalf: but yet I would have you wise unto that which is good, and simple concerning evil" (Romans 16:19).

- "But now is made manifest, and by the scriptures of the prophets, according to the commandment of the everlasting God, **made known to all nations for the obedience of faith**" (Romans 16:26).

- "Let your women keep silence in the churches: for it is not permitted unto them to speak; but they are **commanded to be under obedience**, as also saith the law" (1 Corinthians 14:34).

- "And his inward affection is more abundant toward you, **whilst he remembereth the obedience of you all**, how with fear and trembling ye received him" (2 Corinthians 7:15).

- "Casting down imaginations, and every high thing that exalteth itself against the knowledge of God, and **bringing into captivity every thought to the obedience of Christ**; and having in a readiness to revenge all disobedience, **when your obedience is fulfilled**" (2 Corinthians 10:5–6).
- "Having confidence in thy obedience I wrote unto thee, **knowing that thou wilt also do more than I say**" (Philemon 1:21).
- "Though he were a Son, **yet learned he obedience by the things which he suffered**" (Hebrews 5:8).
- "Elect according to the foreknowledge of God the Father, through sanctification of the Spirit, **unto obedience** and sprinkling of the blood of Jesus Christ: Grace unto you, and peace, be multiplied" (1 Peter 1:2).

In Hebrews 11, the great faith chapter (sometimes called the "Hall of Faith"), those commended for their faith all followed the callings and commands of God **in obedience**. They did not initiate an effort or agenda to do something great for God! As we understand these examples of people who were faithful to God and his work in their lives, we too are exhorted in chapter 12 to "run the race" that God has set before each of us, looking unto Jesus the author and finisher of our faith.

Because OBEDIENCE to the will of God is the issue, we should:

- Learn what is the will of God.

- Understand how to apply the will of God to our lives (This is wisdom, and it is a gift from God as we abide in him.)
- Obey! Do the will of God.

As the songwriter so adequately wrote, "Obedience is the very best way to show that you believe." And remember how Samuel had to remind Saul of this simple truth, "Behold, to obey is better than sacrifice, and to hearken than the fat of rams" (1 Samuel 15:22).

In his book *Changed into His Image*, Jim Berg used the analogy of the education process in his explanation of discipleship. He pointed out that the first lesson a child needs to learn is, "You can't have your own way!" Why? Because it is all too common that "our way" (i.e., "our will") gets in the way of "obedience" to God's will.

It seems to me that this all boils down to a clash of ambition and obedience. We think we can create an agenda to please God, while obedience to God's agenda is what God requires and desires. We determine an outcome that we desire rather than accepting the outcome God desired.

Perhaps some thought-provoking questions would be an effective way to end this narrative. It may set our minds toward meditation on this profound yet simple truth of the importance of obedience. And the better we understand it, the more we will embrace it. How would you answer these?

- How much simpler would life be if one would embrace God's way?

- How different would the judgment seat of Christ be if one would understand and embrace this truth?
- How different would a church congregation look?
- How different would a pastor's work be?
- How much stress and anxiety would disappear?
- How much more joy would one experience?
- How different would family relationships be?
- How much better would a work environment be?
- What does God desire of you? Require of you?
- Keep going! Write out your own questions, thoughts, etc.

Could Jesus have made this issue clearer than his emphatic statement recorded in John 14:15? "If ye love me, keep my commandments." How is it that we love God? Ambition? Doing great things for him? Or is it simple obedience? Just walking in his ways! Pretty obvious, is it not?

CHAPTER 11

A FULFILLED LIFE

I f one were to poll the entire population of America, asking them to define what their ultimate fulfillment in life would be, what do you suppose the list of responses would look like? Would some say, "I have checked off all the boxes on my bucket list"? Would others declare that they had accumulated massive wealth and were living life in luxury and comfort? How would you define ultimate fulfillment?

John was the last living apostle, and by some accounts, John wrote the little letter of 3 John to Gaius, one of his sons in the faith, about AD 90. If that is the case, John had been a follower of Jesus Christ for nearly six decades, most of that after Jesus ascended into heaven. In the fourth verse, John makes an incredible statement.

Beloved, I wish above all things that thou mayest prosper and be in health, even as thy soul prospereth.

For I rejoiced greatly, when the brethren came and testified of the truth that is in thee, even as thou walkest in the truth. **I have no greater joy than to hear that my children walk in truth.** 3 John 1:2–4

Now stop and think about that last sentence for a minute. Think about what John was saying! He said that this world had nothing to offer that would bring about more joy in his life, than to hear that those he had influenced for Christ were continuing in life with their faith in God's Word. Isn't that wonderful? To me, that is the picture of a fulfilled life. Ultimately, it says, "Your life mattered!" You did the work that God gave you to do! You dressed and kept your little garden in Eden!

This is exactly what Jesus Christ wants for us. Speaking as the vine and us as the branches, Jesus said this:

As the Father hath loved me, so have I loved you: continue ye in my love. If ye keep my commandments, ye shall abide in my love; even as I have kept my Father's commandments, and abide in his love. **These things have I spoken unto you, that my joy might remain in you, and that your joy might be full.** John 15:9–11

In his second epistle, John, understanding that the enemies of God would try to distract us and derail our walk with God, wrote:

For many deceivers are entered into the world, who confess not that Jesus Christ is come in the flesh. This is a deceiver and an antichrist. Look to yourselves, that we lose not those things which we have wrought, but that we receive a full reward. 2 John 1:7–8

The Apostle Paul offered up some encouraging words and thoughts as he neared the end of his life and ministry. He confidently declared:

For I am now ready to be offered, and the time of my departure is at hand. **I have fought a good fight, I have finished my course, I have kept the faith**: Henceforth there is laid up for me a crown of righteousness, which the Lord, the righteous judge, shall give me at that day: and not to me only, but unto all them also that love his appearing. 2 Timothy 4:6–8

And finally, Jesus Christ, in his great high priestly prayer, said:

I have glorified thee on the earth: I have finished the work which thou gavest me to do. And now, O Father, glorify thou me with thine own self with the glory which I had with thee before the world was. John 17:4–5

Is the common thread obvious to you? Do you see what each of these men understood about life and fulfillment? They understood that life was all about knowing God, finding, and doing the will of God. And this is what life is about for you and me. They tended their little gardens of paradise—to the glory of God the Father. And we each have a little garden in Eden to tend as well. That is what brings God pleasure and delight. That is what doing the will of God looks like for you. This is where you will find personal fulfillment, the fullness of joy, and the abundant life God desires for you!

As we bring this writing to a close, here are some summary thoughts upon which we can meditate.

- As true believers, we have a relationship with the living God.
- We have been saved from sin **by a person**, reconciled **to a person** (God), to have a **living**, **growing relationship** with him.
- God is at work in our lives, and **he** is conforming us to the image of his dear Son.
- God has initiated the process of reconciling us and recreating us in righteousness and true holiness through sanctification. We have not been saved to become religious! **He wants us to be in a sweet relationship with him.**
- God has given us new life, adopted us into his family, made us alive in Christ, and has indwelled us with

his Holy Spirit **so we can have this everlasting relationship with him**.

- **We worship God from the heart as we love him and seek to please him,** not to impress others or gain the praise of man!
- **We have the privilege of going directly to him in prayer.** We look to hear directly from him from his Word with the help of the Holy Spirit of God!
- We have not been saved to be secluded, **we have been saved to serve him, to magnify him, and to glorify him**.
- As salt and light, we have **a public work**, our unique platforms (our gardens), and we have **a personal and private walk** with the Lord!

Don't complicate the simplicity of a relationship with God. King Solomon said, "Let us hear the conclusion of the whole matter: **Fear God, and keep his commandments: for this is the whole duty of man.** For God shall bring every work into judgment, with every secret thing, whether it be good, or whether it be evil" (Ecclesiastes 12:13–14).

As Micah the prophet confronted Israel, God's people, about their controversy with God, the prophet explains how they were to get right with God and stay right:

Wherewith shall I come before the Lord, and bow myself before the high God? shall I come before him with burnt offerings, with calves of a year old? [Religious practice.] Will the Lord be pleased with thousands of rams, or with ten thousands of rivers of oil? shall I give my firstborn for my transgression, the fruit of my body for the sin of my soul? [Religious works.] He hath shewed thee, O man, what is good; and **what doth the Lord require of thee**, but to **do justly**, and to **love mercy**, and to walk humbly with thy God? Micah 6:6–8

I truly hope that you will find your own little garden in Eden, and you dress it and keep it as the Lord directs your life. When we occupy our garden and obey the Lord, we find peace and joy while looking one day to be called home to the Master's garden. This is our blessed hope!

ABOUT THE AUTHOR

DR. MIKE DUFFY and his wife of fifty-six years have three children together, twelve grandchildren, and five great-grandchildren. Mike's life experience is characterized by service, integrity, leadership, and accomplishment. He grew up in a home that was shattered by alcoholism when he was in elementary school. Overcoming this tragedy and trauma early in life, he has experienced productivity and success on many levels.

Mike is a combat veteran who served a tour in Vietnam with an infantry battalion of the United States Army's Eighty-Second Airborne Division. He learned early the value and reward of working hard and excelled in a corporate career for fourteen years in administrative management and sales, receiving international awards at each level for outstanding achievement and accomplishment.

Dr. Duffy received Jesus Christ as his personal Savior at age thirty-one and committed his life to Christian ministry at age thirty-five, ministering God's Word in nearly one thousand ministries nationally and internationally.

The following statement from Mike reveals his heart:

"There is trauma and tragedy everywhere. I believe that everyone will face some adversity in life. How one responds to that adversity will shape their future. People can be paralyzed, damaged, or destroyed when adversity comes, or they can use adversity as motivation for positive change. We cannot change the past, but we do not have to live there either. We must learn from the past, look toward the future, but live today. Although no one can go back and change their beginning, they can begin today to change their ending. This is what hope looks like. I love serving God and others and have found that this approach in life is the pathway to happiness."

Mike has authored several books and hundreds of articles in his *My Library of Life* which can be found on his website: www.drmikeduffy.com.

ENDNOTES

1. Strong's Hebrew Lexicon, "H376," Blue Letter Bible, accessed March 15, 2025, https://www.blueletterbible.org/lexicon/h376/kjv/wlc/0-1/.

2. Strong's Hebrew Lexicon, "H802," Blue Letter Bible, accessed March 15, 2025, https://www.blueletterbible.org/lexicon/h802/kjv/wlc/0-1/.

3. Strong's Hebrew Lexicon, "H1588," Blue Letter Bible, accessed March 15, 2025, https://www.blueletterbible.org/lexicon/h1588/kjv/wlc/0-1.

4. Strong's Hebrew Lexicon, "H5731," Blue Letter Bible, accessed March 15, 2025, https://www.blueletterbible.org/lexicon/h5731/kjv/wlc/0-1/.

5. Strong's Greek Lexicon, "G2107," Blue Letter Bible, accessed March 15, 2025, https://www.blueletterbible.org/lexicon/g2107/kjv/tr/0-1/.

6. Strong's Greek Lexicon, "G266," Blue Letter Bible, accessed March 15, 2025, https://www.blueletterbible.org/lexicon/g266/kjv/tr/0-1/.

7. Strong's Greek Lexicon, "G2288," Blue Letter Bible, accessed March 15, 2025, https://www.blueletterbible.org/lexicon/g2288/kjv/tr/0-1/.

8. Strong's Hebrew Lexicon, "H4191," Blue Letter Bible, accessed March 15, 2025, https://www.blueletterbible.org/lexicon/h4191/kjv/wlc/0-1/.

9. Strong's Hebrew Lexicon, "H7939," Blue Letter Bible, accessed March 15, 2025, https://www.blueletterbible.org/lexicon/h7939/kjv/wlc/0-1/.

10. Robert Smith, "True Repentance," Quote Fancy, accessed March 15, 2025, https://quotefancy.com/quote/1419915/Robert-Smith-True-repentance-has-a-double-aspect-It-looks-upon-things-past-with-a-weeping.

11. Strong's Greek Lexicon, "G4893," Blue Letter Bible, accessed March 15, 2025, https://www.blueletterbible.org/lexicon/g4893/kjv/tr/0-1/.

12. Nancy Leigh DeMoss, ed., *The Rebirth of America* (Philadelphia: Arthur S. DeMoss Foundation, 1986), 41, https://archive.org/details/rebirthofamerica00arth/mode/2up.

13. David Cloud, "Men Who Were Converted Trying to Disprove the Bible, Part 1 of 3," Way of Life Literature, April 4, 2017, https://www.wayoflife.org/reports/men-who-were-converted-disprove-bible-pt1.php.

14. Strong's Greek Lexicon, "G862," Blue Letter Bible, accessed March 15, 2025, https://www.blueletterbible.org/lexicon/g862/kjv/tr/0-1/.

15. Strong's Greek Lexicon, "G283," Blue Letter Bible, accessed March 15, 2025, https://www.blueletterbible.org/lexicon/g283/kjv/tr/0-1/.

16. Strong's Greek Lexicon, "G263," Blue Letter Bible, accessed March 15, 2025, https://www.blueletterbible.org/lexicon/g263/kjv/tr/0-1/.

17. See Ephesians 4:11, https://www.blueletterbible.org/kjv/eph/4/11/s_1101011.

18. Strong's Greek Lexicon, "G3076," Blue Letter Bible, accessed March 15, 2025, https://www.blueletterbible.org/lexicon/g3076/kjv/tr/0-1/.

19. American Heritage Dictionary, "Principle," accessed March 2, 2025, https://ahdictionary.com/word/search.html?q=principles.

20. Strong's Greek Lexicon, "G3431," Blue Letter Bible, accessed March 15, 2025, https://www.blueletterbible.org/lexicon/g3431/kjv/tr/0-1/.

21. Strong's Greek Lexicon, "G4202," Blue Letter Bible, accessed March 15, 2025, https://www.blueletterbible.org/lexicon/g4202/kjv/tr/0-1/.

22. Strong's Greek Lexicon, "G167," Blue Letter Bible, accessed March 15, 2025, https://www.blueletterbible.org/lexicon/g167/kjv/tr/0-1/.

23. Strong's Greek Lexicon, "G766," Blue Letter Bible, accessed March 15, 2025, https://www.blueletterbible.org/lexicon/g766/kjv/tr/0-1/.

24. Strong's Greek Lexicon, "G1495," Blue Letter Bible, accessed March 15, 2025, https://www.blueletterbible.org/lexicon/g1495/kjv/tr/0-1/.

25. Strong's Greek Lexicon, "G5331," Blue Letter Bible, accessed March 15, 2025, https://www.blueletterbible.org/lexicon/g5331/kjv/tr/0-1/.

26. Strong's Greek Lexicon, "G2189," Blue Letter Bible, accessed March 15, 2025, https://www.blueletterbible.org/lexicon/g2189/kjv/tr/0-1/.

27. Strong's Greek Lexicon, "G2054," Blue Letter Bible, accessed March 15, 2025, https://www.blueletterbible.org/lexicon/g2054/kjv/tr/0-1/.

28. Strong's Greek Lexicon, "G2205," Blue Letter Bible, accessed March 15, 2025, https://www.blueletterbible.org/lexicon/g2205/kjv/tr/0-1/.

29. Strong's Greek Lexicon, "G2372," Blue Letter Bible, accessed March 15, 2025, https://www.blueletterbible.org/lexicon/g2372/kjv/tr/0-1/.

30. Strong's Greek Lexicon, "G2052," Blue Letter Bible, accessed March 15, 2025, https://www.blueletterbible.org/lexicon/g2052/kjv/tr/0-1/.

31. Strong's Greek Lexicon, "G1370," Blue Letter Bible, accessed March 15, 2025, https://www.blueletterbible.org/lexicon/g1370/kjv/tr/0-1/.

32. Strong's Greek Lexicon, "G139," Blue Letter Bible, accessed March 15, 2025, https://www.blueletterbible.org/lexicon/g139/kjv/tr/0-1/.

33. Strong's Greek Lexicon, "G5355," Blue Letter Bible, accessed March 15, 2025, https://www.blueletterbible.org/lexicon/g5355/kjv/tr/0-1/.

34. Strong's Greek Lexicon, "G5408," Blue Letter Bible, accessed March 15, 2025, https://www.blueletterbible.org/lexicon/g5408/kjv/tr/0-1/.

35. Strong's Greek Lexicon, "G3178," Blue Letter Bible, accessed March 15, 2025, https://www.blueletterbible.org/lexicon/g3178/kjv/tr/0-1/.

36. Strong's Greek Lexicon, "G2970," Blue Letter Bible, accessed March 15, 2025, https://www.blueletterbible.org/lexicon/g2970/kjv/tr/0-1/.

37. Strong's Greek Lexicon, "G3664," Blue Letter Bible, accessed March 15, 2025, https://www.blueletterbible.org/lexicon/g3664/kjv/tr/0-1/.

38. Strong's Greek Lexicon, "G26," Blue Letter Bible, accessed

March 15, 2025, https://www.blueletterbible.org/lexicon/g26/kjv/tr/0-1/.

39. Strong's Greek Lexicon, "G5479," Blue Letter Bible, accessed March 15, 2025, https://www.blueletterbible.org/lexicon/g5479/kjv/tr/0-1/.

40. Strong's Greek Lexicon, "G1515," Blue Letter Bible, accessed March 15, 2025, https://www.blueletterbible.org/lexicon/g1515/kjv/tr/0-1/.

41. Strong's Greek Lexicon, "G3115," Blue Letter Bible, accessed March 15, 2025, https://www.blueletterbible.org/lexicon/g3115/kjv/tr/0-1/.

42. Strong's Greek Lexicon, "G5544," Blue Letter Bible, accessed March 15, 2025, https://www.blueletterbible.org/lexicon/g5544/kjv/tr/0-1/.

43. Strong's Greek Lexicon, "G19," Blue Letter Bible, accessed March 15, 2025, https://www.blueletterbible.org/lexicon/g19/kjv/tr/0-1/.

44. Strong's Greek Lexicon, "G4102," Blue Letter Bible, accessed March 15, 2025, https://www.blueletterbible.org/lexicon/g4102/kjv/tr/0-1/.

45. Strong's Greek Lexicon, "G4236," Blue Letter Bible, accessed March 15, 2025, https://www.blueletterbible.org/lexicon/g4236/kjv/tr/0-1/.

46. Strong's Greek Lexicon, "G1466," Blue Letter Bible, accessed March 15, 2025, https://www.blueletterbible.org/lexicon/g1466/kjv/tr/0-1/.

47. Strong's Greek Lexicon, "G1909," Blue Letter Bible, accessed March 15, 2025, https://www.blueletterbible.org/lexicon/g1909/kjv/tr/0-1/.

48. Strong's Greek Lexicon, "G2821," Blue Letter Bible, accessed March 15, 2025, https://www.blueletterbible.org/lexicon/g2821/kjv/tr/0-1/.

49. See Ephesians 5:15, https://www.blueletterbible.org/kjv/eph/5/15/t_conc_1102015; Strong's Greek Lexicon, "G199," Blue Letter Bible, accessed March 15, 2025, https://www.blueletterbible.org/lexicon/g199/kjv/tr/0-1/.

50. Strong's Greek Lexicon, "G4336," Blue Letter Bible, accessed March 15, 2025, https://www.blueletterbible.org/lexicon/g4336/kjv/tr/0-1/.

51. Strong's Greek Lexicon, "G89," Blue Letter Bible, accessed March 15, 2025, https://www.blueletterbible.org/lexicon/g89/kjv/tr/0-1/.

52. Strong's Hebrew Lexicon, "H6588," Blue Letter Bible, accessed March 15, 2025, https://www.blueletterbible.org/lexicon/h6588/kjv/wlc/0-1/.

53. Strong's Hebrew Lexicon, "H5771," Blue Letter Bible, accessed March 15, 2025, https://www.blueletterbible.org/lexicon/h5771/kjv/wlc/0-1/.

54. Strong's Hebrew Lexicon, "H2403," Blue Letter Bible, accessed March 15, 2025, https://www.blueletterbible.org/lexicon/h2403/kjv/wlc/0-1/.

55. Strong's Greek Lexicon, "G659," Blue Letter Bible, accessed March 15, 2025, https://www.blueletterbible.org/lexicon/g659/kjv/tr/0-1/.

56. Strong's Greek Lexicon, "G365," Blue Letter Bible, accessed March 15, 2025, https://www.blueletterbible.org/lexicon/g365/kjv/tr/0-1/.